Warman's®

KISS

Collectibles

FIELD GUIDE

Tom Shannon

Values and Identification

Published by

700 East State Street • Iola, WI 54990-0001
715-445-2214 • 888-457-2873

Our toll-free number to place an order or obtain a free catalog is (800) 258-0929.

Library of Congress Catalog Number: 2005924834

ISBN: 0-89689-221-2

Designed by Donna Mummery
Edited by Kristine Manty

Printed in the United States of America

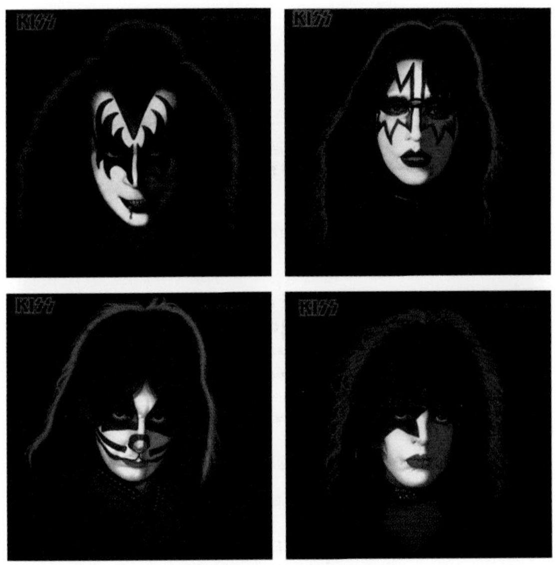

The covers of each KISS members' solo album.
Prices for Gene Simmons' album are on P. 380, the rest are on P. 383.

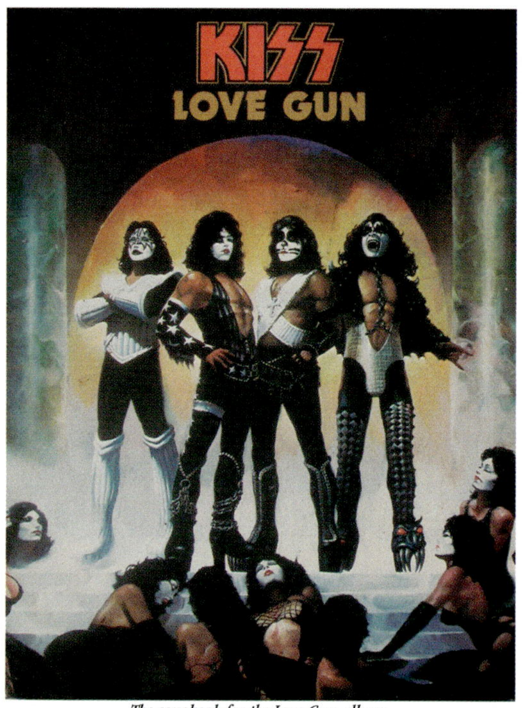

The songbook for the Love Gun album.
Prices can be found on P. 77.

Contents

Acknowledgments 6

Introduction 9

Price Guide 30

American and Selected Foreign Music 345

Albums 364

45 Singles and Extended Plays 425

An Interview with Bill Aucoin 490

Index 508

Acknowledgments

This book is dedicated to the two most important people in my life: my wife Tammy and my daughter Jennifer. You both make my life complete.

I must thank many people, without whom I never would have learned what I have about the world of KISS collecting.

For contributing to my education during the formative years of my introduction to KISS collecting, I thank the following: Gary Conn, Tim McGuire, Michael Fortenberry, and Francis O'Hara. Francis probably taught me more than anyone, and I owe him a big thanks. Francis, my hand is always extended if you want to take it. Thanks again Estil Robinson for your outstanding photography. A special thanks to Steve Sizemore and Bret Parker for letting me hang out with (oops I forgot; I mean *roadie* for) SSG at the KISS conventions.

A great number of people contributed information and photos for inclusion in this book. Most of your photos will appear on the KISS collectors' Web site www.kisshall.com. Thank you: Frank Aqualina, Jeff Barre, Tom Beattie, Michael Gangnuss, Lee Gibbert, Steve Glastetter, Julian Gill and www.kissfaq.com, Scott Harloff, Mike Holland, Colin Humphrey, Vladimir Iliyn, Luis Jimenez-

Trevino, Lloyd Kellett, Dale Kemp, James Kershaw, KISS Hell and Joe Degraffenreid, Frank King, Hugo Koch, Amadeo Lopez, Dave Massie, Brett Meyer, Esteban Tres Morata, Daniel Mueller, Rick Reese, Sean Reid, Frank Romeo, Mark Sawatzky, Brian Singer, Garrison Spick, Kevin Taylor, John Henry and Tiffany Thomas, Cesare Vallesi, Rich Vanderwerken, Wayne Wajda.

Thank you to all of the following corporations and entities that provide information and/or materials for this edition: Big Bang distributors and Ahead Drum sticks, Art Asylum, D'Andrea guitar picks, Dark Horse comics and Lee Dawson, DW Drums, Fun 4 All, Gibson Guitars and Jeff Ivester, www.kissshop.com, www.kissasylum.com, www.kissmuseum.com, Ken Rodenas' outstanding picks and sticks page at www.kissonline.com, NECA, Signatures Network, Bill Henshell and Washburn International, and the best source for KISS picks on the planet, Jeff Stouder at tjtraders@aol.com. A huge thanks to the following for providing information, materials and access: Keith Leroux at the KISS Shop, Bill Aucoin, Bruce Kulick and Lydia Criss.

Obviously, thanks also to Paul Stanley, Gene Simmons, Peter Criss, and Ace Frehley for forming KISS.

The band's debut album, KISS, released in February 1974. Values for this album are on P. 362.

Introduction

You Wanted the Best...You Got the Best...The Hottest Band in the Land...KISS!!!

Instantly upon hearing these words, strong images develop in even the most casual fan's brain. Demonic bassist Gene Simmons hunkers above the concert stage light trusses, blood oozing from between his snarled lips. Star Child singer/guitarist Paul Stanley struts across the stage, controlling the enraptured crowd with his every move. Cat Man Peter Criss commands thunder from his levitating drum kit. Smoke bellows from the seemingly possessed guitar of the Space Man Ace Frehley. How did this imagery come to be so deeply ingrained? As is typically the case in an iconic band's formation, calculated design and a series of incidents that can only be looked back on as sheer luck, paved the way.

A band is born

The origins of KISS can be traced to a frosty 1968 encounter in Queens, N.Y. Gene Simmons (Gene Klein at that time) and Stanley Eisen (destined to be Paul Stanley) met for the first time at the home of a mutual friend. Despite their initial personality conflicts, they eventually formed a lifelong bond and came to recognize and respect the other's unwavering drive to succeed. This resolute respect became the basis of a 30-year relationship that can best be equated to that of birth brothers.

Embracing their common goals, Gene and Stanley joined forces in several bands that transformed over the course of personnel changes into Wicked Lester. By 1972, Wicked Lester seemed on the surface to be everything the newly renamed Gene Simmons and Paul Stanley could have ever hoped. They signed with Epic records, recorded their debut LP, and even had the artwork picked out for the release (check out the cover art at www.kisshall.com), yet something was wrong. Simmons and Stanley realized that Wicked Lester just did not have "IT." They had a lead guitarist who wanted to sit when he played, and they used flutes in songs. Upon hearing the songs recorded by Wicked Lester, available on the KISS box set, an honest observer has to marvel at the ability of Simmons and Stanley to completely change their song writing styles to write what would become the first KISS album. By any standard, that entire album has withstood the test of time. The same cannot be said for Wicked Lester.

In mid-1972, Simmons and Stanley fired the rest of the band and recruited drummer Peter Criscoula (Peter Criss) into Wicked Lester. The trio attempted to retain the Epic records agreement. They performed Wicked Lester and early KISS songs live in white face makeup for an Epic representative, who was entirely unimpressed. The contract was cancelled. Undaunted, they continued practicing as a trio until December when they were joined by lead guitarist Paul Frehley. Since the band already had a resident Paul, Frehley quickly changed his name to Ace, and the band was complete.

Great expectations

For the next 10 months, KISS members spent all of their resources and energy perfecting their sound and show. Their first concert on January 30, 1973 revealed little of what was to come. The makeup was nonexistent, the stage cramped, and the crowd could most likely have been counted on one hand. By March, the makeup began to evolve. On August 10, young TV producer Bill Aucoin, clutching a handmade concert pass, sat in the audience at The Hotel Diplomat as KISS blew the audience away. Aucoin immediately signed the band to a management contract. By mid-November, KISS was in Bell Sound studios in Manhattan recording their

After hitting a rough patch, the live double album, Alive!, put the band and its record company Casablanca back on the map. Alive! LP with gold certification sticker. Values of this album are on P. 365.

debut LP for Neil Bogart and his brand new record label, Casablanca.

KISS was released in February 1974. The band spent the next 12 months recording albums and performing throughout North America. One particularly tough five-week period saw KISS perform shows from Alaska to Florida. Hotter than Hell was recorded during touring down time in August, and KISS was back on the road from October to February 1975. How did the band celebrate the end of this 12-month journey? By entering the studio once more to record Dressed to Kill, and hitting the highways again.

While the band stayed productive, problems were rising threateningly on the horizon. Despite the fact the band was periodically drawing crowds in excess of 10,000, all was not well in the KISS camp. According to Bill Aucoin, the first three albums were only selling in the neighborhood of 30,000 units each, and then fading. Casablanca was faltering financially, and had yet to pay the band any substantial royalties. Something had to be done to build a buzz and capture the raw power of KISS live, something that would translate into sales, or the band would most likely have to leave Casablanca records. That was an option Aucoin did not take pleasure in embracing. Even if Casablanca founder Bogart was flying by the seat of his pants financially, Aucoin knew that he was also the band's biggest supporter. He sensed he would never find another record executive who would believe in, and back, the band to the level Bogart would, even if he had not paid them yet. Plans were quickly laid out to produce a two-disc live album, an album that would make or break Casablanca Records.

September 1975 saw KISS hit the road and essentially not stop touring for 19 months. It also marked the debut of the most successful live recording ever released up to that time: KISS Alive! brought the sight and spectacle of a live KISS show to fans' turntables. Including a bonus concert booklet, Alive! also began the era of KISS including inserts in their LPs. The band and Casablanca records were saved.

In 1976, massive hits started coming with regularity. A few days of recording sessions were squeezed into the schedule in between touring dates. The huge selling, experimental sounding Destroyer in March 1976 was followed by a July re-release of the first three albums, titled The Originals. Sales of The Originals were applied to the sales figures of the initial releases, pushing all three over the Gold standard of 500,000 each. Rock and Roll Over was unveiled in November, capping a year of sales that any band would envy. Suddenly everything KISS touched turned to gold.

Love Gun was a top album in 1977. Values of this album are on P. 372.

Released in 1978, Double Platinum was a big hit with fans. Values of this album are on P. 378.

Love Gun and Alive II both had mammoth sales in 1977. Although fans would not realize it for years, 1977 saw the end to classic KISS in many ways. The original members would never record as equal partners again. Everyone participated on Love Gun, but Ace Frehley had no part in the studio side of Alive II. To this day, so many guitarists were used that they cannot seem to agree among themselves who played what. KISS toured successfully until May 1978, but things went down gradually over many years for KISS from this point.

Double Platinum hit stores in April 1978. A compilation of hits, plus a reworking of "Strutter," the album was well received by fans. It also gave the members time to work on the TV movie, "KISS Meets the Phantom of the Park," as well as their solo album projects. A project the scope of the solo albums was unprecedented: four simultaneously released albums, each one providing a look into the soul of each member. All four shipped Platinum. All four together experienced one of the biggest documented return rates in the history of music retailing. More than four million LPs pressed and shipped. You have to wonder what the executives were thinking. Suddenly KISS solo records were showing up in discount cut out bins.

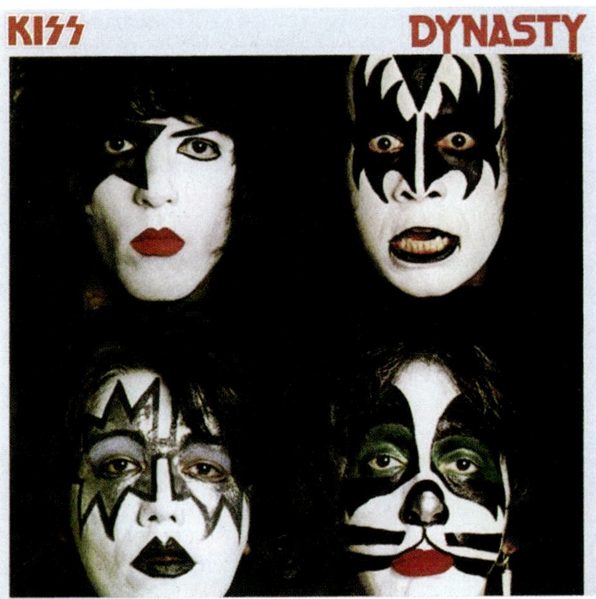

Dynasty, released in May 1979, is an album from KISS' "Super Hero" period. Values for this album can be found on P. 384.

Hard times

Dynasty was released in May 1979, featuring all four members' faces on the cover. Much had changed on a number of levels. The unseen costumes were the most over the top and garish KISS had ever worn—the word "Vegas" quickly comes to mind. The music was not typical KISS. There was very little rock, but a lot of pop and disco. Peter Criss is reported to have only played on one track. All of this was followed by an ambitiously designed and executed concert tour that still managed to bleed money. The underlying business concept was to play multiple nights in cities to cut down on the road expenses. Unfortunately they were not able to sell out single nights. On a more ominous note, as older fans looked around they saw families and children in the crowd. KISS was swiftly perceived as no longer being cool.

One year later, KISS released Unmasked. The music was an even lighter brand of pop than Dynasty and was universally rejected by the KISS Army. Peter Criss was on the cover art, but he had already left the band. Eric Carr was recruited to take his place behind the drum kit in the guise of The Fox. A 41-show tour of Europe and Australia followed. On December 3, 1980, Ace Frehely played his last concert with KISS for 16 years.

KISS was falling precipitously in popularity, but was getting ready to pick up some speed. An ill-conceived concept album, Music From The Elder, was released in November 1981. To this date, it remains the only KISS album of all new material to never be certified Gold. No tour was undertaken in support of the release, and PolyGram records had the band quickly record some new tracks for inclusion on a compilation release for all markets except America. These harder rocking tunes on 1982's KISS Killers showed KISS was serious about returning to their roots. The question became, would it be too late?

The answer came in October 1982. Creatures of the Night was the hardest KISS album since Love Gun five years before. The drums of Eric Carr were phenomenal. With the addition of new lead guitarist Vinnie Vincent, the song writing was first rate, but it was too late. Although many fans today count this as their favorite KISS release, the sales initially were dismal. The concert tour did well to draw 5,000 fans in arenas that once sold 15,000 for a KISS show a few years before. It was time to retool the band.

September 18, 1983 saw the unveiling of makeup-era KISS on MTV. In an event that was covered on network evening news, the band appeared without makeup in public for the first time to promote Lick It Up. The additional airplay pushed the band back to new levels of success. The

Smashes Thrashes and Hits was a new incarnation of KISS. Values of this album can be found on P. 407.

temperamental Vincent was replaced on 1984's Animalize by California guitarist Mark St. John, who promptly contracted a debilitating hand problem at the onset of the tour. He was replaced by long time KISS associate Bruce Kulick, who proved to be a strong, talented, and stable member of KISS over the next decade.

The hits piled up from 1984 to 1990 for this incarnation of KISS. Asylum, Crazy Nights, Smashes Thrashes and Hits, and Hot in the Shade were all great sellers. The band's tours were selling in respectable numbers. Everything seemed well until tragedy struck. After fighting a malignant heart tumor beginning in May, drummer Eric Carr died of a brain hemorrhage on November 24, 1991. His place behind the drum kit was turned over to Eric Singer.

From 1992-1996, the fortunes of KISS began to fade again. Revenge and Alive III appeared to be the last major label releases by KISS. Concert attendance figures plummeted. In 1994, Paul and Gene produced their own tribute album to KISS titled KISS My Ass. The album showcased many top rock, grunge, and country acts performing KISS tunes. This brought validity to the band, but they were unable to capitalize; 1994 and 1995 were marked by condensed tours of South America, and Japan. Soon the band was playing at official KISS conventions in Australia and America. Only the brightest optimist would

Released in the late 1990s, You Wanted the Best You Got the Best marked a return of KISS at the top of their game again. Values for this album can be found on P. 411.

not predict the end seemed near for the band, but things turned around again.

June 17, 1995 found the band performing the first American KISS convention in Burbank, California. Peter Criss contacted Gene Simmons before the show to ask if he could bring his daughter by to see the displays since she was not born when her dad was in the band. This led to Peter singing with the band for two songs at that show. As the convention tour wound its way around the country over the next two months, the Bad Boys tour of Ace Frehley and Peter Criss was doing the same. When KISS recorded an MTV Unplugged show, they asked two special guests to appear: Ace Frehley and Peter Criss.

June 28, 1996 found the reunited KISS standing in full makeup and Love Gun-era costumes before 40,000 screaming fans on a stage in Detroit's Tiger Stadium. It was opening night for a 13-month 192-date sold-out tour of 23 countries. The album, You Wanted the Best, was released. Tours followed in 1998 in support of the album Psycho Circus, 2000 on The (supposed) Farewell Tour, 2003 World Domination with Aerosmith, and 2004 Rock the Nation.

Where will KISS go from here? Much remains in flux in the world of KISS today. Paul Stanley has undergone two recent hip replacement surgeries. Can he strut across the stage with a stainless steel ball joint? Even more importantly, should he? Ace Frehley has left the band of his own free will. Long time band road manager Tommy Thayer, who, interestingly enough, used to be an Ace impersonator in KISS tribute bands in the early 1990s, is attempting to fill his shoes. Eric Singer is once again pounding the drums since Peter Criss is also no longer a member of the band. Gene is busy being a mogul.

Whatever happens, just close your eyes and remember: You Wanted The Best...You Got The Best...The Hottest Band In the Land...KISS!!!

How prices are determined

Prices in the guide reflect the prevailing rate you should expect to pay when purchasing an item in the secondary market. Generally a new item still available for retail purchase will hover near the manufacturer's suggested retail price. Some items that are collecting dust on the shelves will be less. Conversely, items that are disappearing from shelves quickly will be priced at a premium. Memorabilia no longer available for retail sale is of course obtainable only in the secondary market.

These prices are not indicative of what a collector can sell an item to a dealer for, but they should be accurate for collector-to-collector sales and trades. Dealers will generally pay 30 percent to 50 percent of book price. Analysis of collectors' magazine ads and auction results, dealer's sales lists and postings, and a board of KISS collectors, determined prevailing prices. Prices are not being set for KISS collectibles, but current tendencies are being reported. These prices are not to be construed as an offer by the author to purchase. (Except the Blue label stock copy of Let Me Go, Rock and Roll/Hotter Than Hell. I am offering to buy that!)

Condition grading

The grading system I use consists of Poor (P), Very Good (VG), Excellent (EX), Near Mint (NM), and Mint (M). Too often people use + and - signs in addition to these grades. You will probably rarely encounter anything that is Mint, as most items experience some sort of shelf or shipping wear. That is why the price guide lists NM as the top grade priced. Boxes and covers of items can have a completely different grade from their contents. The following grading system may be considered as a guide. Not all things need be present to fit the grade.

- M–Case fresh, absolutely mint, no creases, never had a price sticker.

- NM–Slight imperfections in packaging, slight shelf wear, some loss of shine.

- EX–Slight creases, slight scuffing, might have evidence of a price sticker.

- VG–Creases that expose bare paper, sticker has peeled off covering.

- P–Window plastic gone, multiple creases, crushed or torn sections.

Why some items are not listed

Other than space limitations, the most important reason is probably because the item is a bootleg or counterfeit item. No bootlegs or counterfeits are listed unless they are so well made that they will cause confusion, especially among new collectors.

What is the difference between a bootleg and a counterfeit? A *bootleg* is an item that has not been authorized by KISS to be manufactured. Examples would be an Ace Frehley lunch box, Eric Carr Mego doll, Live concert recordings, and live video tapes. Quality is usually not up to par on concert bootlegs. Live CDs will have crowd noise, live video tapes will have picture fade and hiss. Some memorabilia bootlegs are quite well done. Those are the ones I try to mention in the book–not to legitimize them, but to educate collectors that an item is not authentic. A *counterfeit* is any item that is manufactured to replicate a legitimate KISS authorized item. These are generally rare CDs, posters, and tour merchandise. Counterfeits are manufactured and sold by thieves, plain and simple. They are produced only to rip off the band, and more so collectors. Some of the more common counterfeit items include guitar picks, older Peter Criss drumsticks, and vintage boxes. The number of counterfeit Mego doll boxes have become so overwhelming that the values for real boxes have plummeted.

One final reason an item might not be in the book is because it is an item manufactured or sold in a foreign country. I collected materials from fans around the world for this book, including an unbelievable amount of 1980 Australian merchandise. There is only so much room in this edition, so the line had to be drawn somewhere. Luckily, everything that did not make it into the book will become available to view at the worldwide KISS collectors Web site: www.kisshall.com.

There will be more than 280 45 rpm picture sleeves, photos of rare posters, prototypes, and much more. You will also be able to reach me online at that site.

If you know of an item I have missed, you can send any supporting evidence (photographs, photocopies, paperwork, etc.) in a self-addressed stamped envelope to the address below. Documenting evidence will not be returned, so do not send anything you want back. You can reach me online at www.kisshall.com; or you can mail information to me at the following address:

Tom Shannon
P.O. Box 25056
Lexington, KY. 40524

Price Guide

Items manufactured after the release of this book
can be seen at www.kisshall.com.

Item	VG	EX	NM
Action figures			
3-D Animator			
Box of four	$4-5	$8-10	$15-20
Individual boxed	$1-1	$2-2	$3-4

3D Animator, box of four.

Mego Ace and Paul, muscle body.

Item	VG	EX	NM
Mego 1978			
Skinny body (No Peter Criss)			
Boxed	$63-75	$125-150	$250-300
Loose	$23-25	$45-50	$90-100
Muscle body			
Boxed	$63-75	$125-150	$250-300
Loose	$28-31	$55-63	$110-125

Mego Peter and Gene, muscle body.

Mego box.

Item	VG	EX	NM
Mego bootleg			
Vinnie Vincent	$25-29	$50-58	$100-115
Eric Carr	$25-29	$50-58	$100-115
Mego boxes (Warning: Many counterfeits exist.)			
	$40-50	$80-100	$160-200

Item	VG	EX	NM
McFarlane Toys			
NOTE: Action figures no longer sealed on a card are worth the lowest VG price, even if they are mint			
Ace Frehley			
ALIVE!			
Name on pick	$5-6	$10-13	$20-25
No name on pick	$5-6	$10-13	$20-25
Album cover			
Black record showing	$2-2	$3-5	$6-9
Gold record showing	$2-3	$4-5	$7-10
No record showing	$2-2	$3-5	$6-9
Letter base			
Face card	$2-3	$5-6	$9-12
Figure card	$3-4	$6-8	$12-15
Psycho Circus			
With Stilt man	$4-5	$8-9	$15-18
Spencer's exclusive	$3-4	$6-8	$12-15
Psycho Circus Tour edition			
Les Paul guitar	$11-13	$23-25	$45-50
Flying V guitar	$4-5	$8-9	$15-18
Tour Venue edition, w/sticker	$4-5	$8-9	$15-18

Alive action figure of Ace Frehley.

Alive action figure of Peter Criss.

Item	VG	EX	NM
Creatures	$2-3	$4-6	$8-12
Peter Criss			
ALIVE!			
Name on pick	$5-6	$10-13	$20-25
No name on pick	$5-6	$10-13	$20-25
Album cover			
Black record showing	$2-2	$3-5	$6-9
Gold record showing	$2-3	$4-5	$7-10
No record showing	$2-2	$3-5	$6-9
Letter base			
Face card	$2-3	$5-6	$9-12
Figure card	$3-4	$6-8	$12-15
Psycho Circus			
With animal trainer	$1-2	$3-4	$5-8
Spencer's exclusive	$3-4	$6-8	$12-15
Psycho Circus Tour edition	$4-5	$8-10	$15-20
Tour Venue edition, w/sticker	$4-5	$8-9	$15-18

Item	VG	EX	NM
Paul Stanley			
ALIVE!			
Name on pick	$2-3	$4-5	$7-10
No name on pick	$2-3	$4-5	$7-10
Album cover			
Black record showing	$2-2	$3-5	$6-9
Gold record showing	$2-3	$4-5	$7-10
No record showing	$2-2	$3-5	$6-9
Letter base			
Face card	$2-3	$5-6	$9-12
Figure card	$1-2	$3-4	$5-8
Psycho Circus			
With clown	$1-2	$3-4	$5-8
Spencer's exclusive	$3-4	$6-8	$12-15
Psycho Circus Tour edition			
Flying V guitar	$11-13	$23-25	$45-50
Les Paul guitar	$4-5	$8-9	$15-18
Tour Venue edition, w/sticker	$4-5	$8-9	$15-18

Alive action figure of Paul Stanley.

Alive action figure of Gene Simmons.

Item	VG	EX	NM
Creatures	$2-3	$4-6	$8-12
Gene Simmons			
ALIVE!			
Name on pick	$2-3	$4-5	$7-10
No name on pick	$2-3	$4-5	$7-10
With Catman on backing card	$5-6	$10-3	$20-25

A 12-inch Gene Simmons Alive action figure.

Item	VG	EX	NM
12" figure in custom box	$3-4	$6-8	$12-15
Album cover			
Black record showing	$2-3	$4-5	$7-10
Gold record showing	$2-3	$5-6	$9-11
No record showing	$2-3	$4-5	$7-10
Letter base			
Face card	$2-3	$5-6	$9-12

Creatures Gene Simmons' variants.

A 12-inch Gene Simmons Creatures action figure.

Item	VG	EX	NM
Figure card	$3-4	$7-8	$13-16
Blood splattered variant	$6-8	$13-15	$25-30
Psycho Circus			
With ringmaster	$2-3	$5-7	$10-13
Spencer's exclusive	$3-4	$6-8	$12-15
Psycho Circus Tour edition	$2-3	$5-6	$9-12
Tour Venue edition, w/sticker	$4-5	$8-9	$15-18
Creatures	$2-3	$4-6	$8-12
12" figure in custom box	$3-4	$6-8	$12-15
Eric Carr			
Bloody, bare belly variant	$4-5	$8-9	$15-18
Creatures	$2-3	$4-6	$8-12
Boxed multi-figure sets			
ALIVE!	$10-13	$20-25	$40-50
Creatures	$10-13	$20-25	$40-50
Love Gun	$10-13	$20-25	$40-50

Creatures action figures of Ace, Paul, Eric and Gene.

Minimates box set.

Item	VG	EX	NM
Minimates			
Set of 4 on box	$5-6	$10-3	$20-25
Individual packaged	$1-1	$2-3	$3-5

Fun 4 All/Art Asylum 24" figures

(200 of each member's Destroyer figure were autographed on a sticker applied to the box)

(25 of each member's Love Gun figure were autographed on the certificate of authenticity)

Item	VG	EX	NM
Destroyer and Love Gun			
Boxed	$19-25	$38-50	$75-100
Loose	$10-13	$20-25	$40-50

Signed boxes, add $50

Minimates individual packs.

A 24-inch Gene Simmons Love Gun action figure.

A 24-inch Ace Frehley Destroyer action figure.

A 24-inch Paul Stanley Destroyer action figure.

A 24-inch Peter Criss Destroyer action figure.

A 24-inch Gene Simmons Destroyer action figure.

Smiti action figure sets. Note the Spencer Gifts variant in the top set.

Item	VG	EX	NM
Smiti Block Action Figures			
Spencer Gifts Blood Variant	$6-8	$13-15	$25-30
Non-Blood Variant	$5-6	$10-13	$20-25

A 1978 Jaws 2 comic with a back page ad for the second Marvel KISS comic.

Item	VG	EX	NM
Advertisements, full-page magazine			
1974-1976	$2-3	$4-5	$7-10
1977-1983	$1-1	$2-3	$3-5
1983-present	$1-1	$1-2	$1-3
Air freshener			
Love Gun	$1-1	$2-3	$3-5
Rock and Roll Over	$1-1	$2-3	$3-5
Solo Faces	$1-1	$2-3	$3-5

A 1970's-era Dimarzio Pickups Paul Stanley ad.

A 1970's-era Dimarzio Pickups group ad.

Item	VG	EX	NM
Arcade dolls			
26" tall, each	$2-3	$4-5	$7-10
18" tall, each	$1-1	$2-3	$3-5
11" tall, each	$1-1	$2-3	$3-5
Ashtray			
(Many bootlegs exist)			
Black logo with first LP photo	$2-3	$4-5	$7-10
Red logo	$2-3	$4-5	$7-10
Psycho Circus	$2-3	$4-5	$7-10
Autographs			
Eric Carr	$6-8	$13-15	$25-30
Peter Criss	$5-6	$10-13	$20-25
Ace Frehley	$5-6	$10-13	$20-25
Bruce Kulick	$3-4	$5-8	$10-15
Mark St. John	$1-3	$3-5	$5-10
Gene Simmons	$5-6	$10-13	$20-25
Eric Singer	$3-4	$5-8	$10-15
Paul Stanley	$5-6	$10-13	$20-25
Vinnie Vincent	$3-4	$5-8	$10-15
Baby supplies			
Bottle/bib set	$3-4	$6-8	$12-15
Romper outfit	$3-4	$6-8	$12-15

A group of 18-inch Arcade dolls.

The 1978 back pack. Rich Vanderwerken collection.

Item	VG	EX	NM
Backpacks			
Red, group on cubes, 1978			
Sealed	$50-56	$100-113	$200-225
Loose	$19-25	$38-50	$75-100
KISS Army, green	$9-13	$18-25	$35-50

A backstage pass for the Psycho Circus tour, 1998-99.

Item	VG	EX	NM
Backstage pass			
1974-1982	$4-5	$8-10	$15-20
1983-1995	$3-4	$6-8	$12-15
Alive III (Promotional autograph party pass)	$3-4	$6-8	$12-15
1996-present	$3-4	$6-8	$12-15

Item	VG	EX	NM

Bags

For any bags not mentioned here, see the Australia memorabilia section at www.kisshall.com.

Item	VG	EX	NM
Asylum, from Great Sounds	$2-3	$4-5	$7-10
Solo LP, promo	$3-4	$5-8	$10-15
KISS Army, canvas, olive	$6-8	$13-15	$25-30

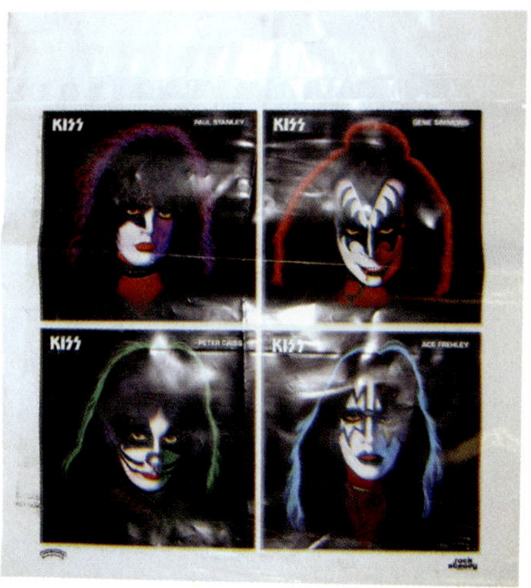

A solo LP shopping bag promo.

KISS baseballs: silver and black, left, and Psycho Circus.

Item	VG	EX	NM
Baseballs			
Psycho Circus or silver and black			
Boxed	$1-2	$3-4	$5-8
Loose	$0-1	$1-2	$1-3

Item	VG	EX	NM
Balloons			
New Years Eve 1996, 5 colors	$1-2	$3-4	$5-8
Solo album (bootleg)	$1-2	$2-3	$3-6
Rock & Roll Over, Mylar, 16"	$3-4	$6-8	$12-15

Balloons from New Year's Eve 1996.

Revenge bandana. Jeff Barre Collection.

Item	VG	EX	NM
Bandanas			
Animalize, black w/ white logo	$1-3	$3-5	$5-10
KISS Army	$1-3	$3-5	$5-10
Revenge	$1-3	$3-5	$5-10
Rock and Roll Over, 1977	$6-8	$13-15	$25-30
Rock and Roll Over, 1998	$1-3	$3-5	$5-10
Psycho Circus	$1-2	$2-4	$4-7

Item	VG	EX	NM
Bean Bag Toys			
Each member			
Boxed	$1-3	$3-5	$5-10
Loose	$1-1	$2-3	$3-5
Psycho Circus wagon with all four beans	$10-13	$20-25	$40-50
Bears			
Love Gun			
Boxed	$19-25	$38-50	$75-100
Loose	$6-8	$13-15	$25-30
Dynasty			
Boxed	$31-38	$63-75	$125-150
Loose	$10-13	$20-25	$40-50

Dynasty bears. Rich Vanderwerken collection.

Love Gun bears.
Jennifer Shannon collection.

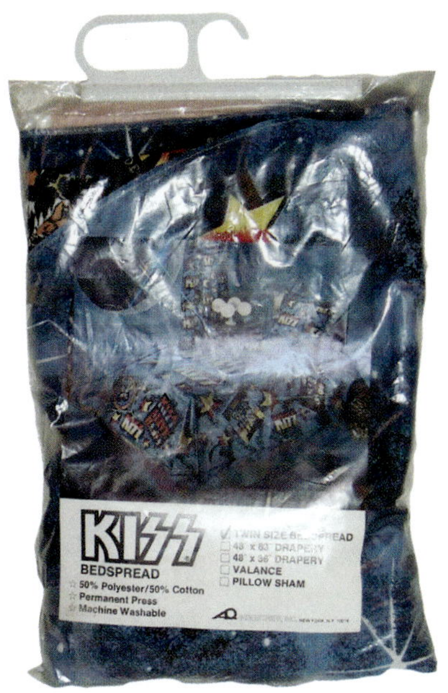

Bedspread in original bag. Rich Vanderwerken collection.

Item	VG	EX	NM
Bed spread			
Sealed	$225-250	$450-500	$900-1,000
Loose	$44-56	$88-113	$175-225

Czechoslovakian beer cans.

Item	VG	EX	NM
Beer can, Czechoslovakia			
Sealed	$9-13	$18-25	$35-50
Empty	$4-5	$8-10	$15-20

A 1970's blue stretch belt. Rich Vanderwerken collection.

Item	VG	EX	NM
Belt, blue stretch	$75-88	$150-175	$300-350

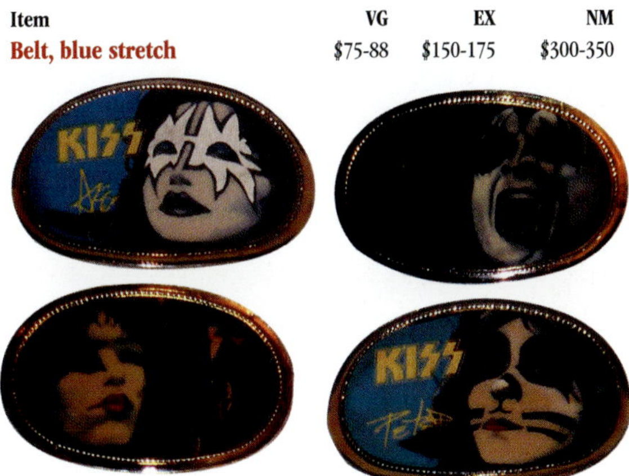

Solo buckles set. Rich Vanderwerken collection.

Belt buckles			
Ace Frehley Love Gun face	$29-31	$58-63	$115-125
Peter Criss Love Gun face	$29-31	$58-63	$115-125
Paul Stanley Love Gun face	$29-31	$58-63	$115-125
Gene Simmons Love Gun face	$29-31	$58-63	$115-125
Brass logo	$9-10	$18-20	$35-40

Gene Simmons buckle. Jeff Barre Collection.

Item	VG	EX	NM
Belt buckles			
Blue prism logo on olive green	$38-40	$75-80	$150-160
Demon boot with logo	$9-10	$18-20	$35-40
Destroyer artwork	$10-13	$20-25	$40-50
Gargoyle	$9-10	$18-20	$35-40
Gold logo w/rainbow on orange	$44-50	$88-100	$175-200
Gold prism logo on black	$9-10	$18-20	$35-40
Gold prism logo w/stars on blue	$9-10	$18-20	$35-40
Lips with logo, brass (may be bootleg)	$9-10	$18-20	$35-40

Item	VG	EX	NM
Belt buckles			
Love Gun artwork	$10-13	$20-25	$40-50
Orange and red logo on black	$5-6	$10-13	$20-25
Pewter logo, from reunion tour	$5-6	$10-13	$20-25
Pewter logo, block background	$5-6	$10-13	$20-25
Platinum logo	$6-10	$13-20	$25-40
Rock And Roll Over artwork	$25-31	$50-63	$100-125
Silver prism logo on black	$9-10	$18-20	$35-40
Silver prism logo on blue	$9-10	$18-20	$35-40
Silver prism logo w/stars on blue	$9-10	$18-20	$35-40
Sterling Silver logo	$75-80	$150-160	$300-320
Unmasked artwork, bootleg	$5-6	$10-13	$20-25
Bendies/Superposables			
(5" tall bendable dolls)			
Carded	$1-1	$1-3	$2-5
Loose	$0-1	$1-1	$1-2
Box set of all four	$4-5	$8-9	$15-18
Blanket/throw			
Dynasty	$8-10	$15-20	$30-40
Faces with icons	$8-10	$15-20	$30-40
Farewell Tour	$8-10	$15-20	$30-40
Icons	$8-10	$15-20	$30-40
KISS Army	$8-10	$15-20	$30-40
Psycho Circus	$8-10	$15-20	$30-40
Solo faces	$8-10	$15-20	$30-40

Bobble heads.

Item	VG	EX	NM
Bobble heads	$3-4	$6-8	$12-15
Bobble heads, mini box set	$4-5	$8-10	$15-20
Books			
Alive Forever	$5-6	$10-13	$20-25
Behind The Mask	$5-6	$10-13	$20-25
Black Diamond	$12-3	$4-5	$7-10
Black Diamond 2	$2-3	$4-5	$7-10
Goldmine KISS Collectibles	$3-4	$6-8	$12-15
Headliners	$4-5	$8-10	$15-20
Hottest Band In The Land, U.K.	$3-4	$6-8	$12-15
Japan 1977 tour photo book	$4-5	$8-10	$15-20
KISS, Robert Duncan	$4-5	$8-10	$15-20
The KISS Album Focus	$4-5	$8-10	$15-20
KISS and Make-Up, Gene Simmons			
Hard back	$5-6	$10-13	$20-25
Paper back	$2-3	$4-5	$7-10
KISS, Shock Rockers	$2-3	$4-5	$7-10
KISS: The Real Story	$9-11	$18-23	$35-45
KISSTORY	$34-40	$68-80	$135-160
KISSTORY II	$34-40	$68-80	$135-160
KISS and Sell	$1-2	$2-3	$3-6
KISS and Tell	$1-2	$2-3	$3-6
KISS Collectibles	$2-3	$4-5	$7-10
KISS Diary	$11-13	$23-25	$45-50
From Dynasty LP order sheet:			
Outtakes, Chip Rock, paperback	$3-4	$6-8	$12-15

Gene Simmons' autobiography, KISS and Make-Up.

KISStory and KISStory II.

KISStory II displays in some fans' KISS rooms.

Item	VG	EX	NM
Outtakes, Chip Rock, hardback	$8-9	$15-18	$30-35
Psycho Circus, trade book	$3-4	$6-8	$12-15
The KISS Years, with card & CD	$1-3	$3-5	$5-10
Still on Fire, Germany	$2-3	$4-5	$7-10
Books, songbooks			
Ace Frehley	$9-10	$18-20	$35-40
Peter Criss	$9-10	$18-20	$35-40
Paul Stanley	$9-10	$18-20	$35-40
Gene Simmons	$9-10	$18-20	$35-40
Alive!, published 1998	$5-6	$10-13	$20-25
Alive II	$11-13	$23-25	$45-50
Alive II, 1980 era cover, UK	$11-13	$23-25	$45-50
Crazy Nights	$5-6	$10-13	$20-25
Destroyer	$9-10	$18-20	$35-40
Double Platinum	$11-13	$23-25	$45-50
Dynasty	$9-10	$18-20	$35-40
Greatest Hits	$6-8	$13-15	$25-30
IMP Presents KISS	$5-6	$10-13	$20-25
KISS Easy Guitar	$8-9	$15-18	$30-35
KISS For Easy Guitar	$2-3	$4-5	$7-10
KISS Guitar School	$4-5	$8-10	$15-20
KISS Guitar Signature Licks	$4-5	$8-10	$15-20
Books, songbooks with CD			
KISS Guitar Styles	$4-5	$8-10	$15-20
KISS The Guitar Collection	$4-5	$8-10	$15-20
KISS Top 10 Hits Easy Guitar	$4-5	$8-10	$15-20
Love Gun	$9-10	$18-20	$35-40

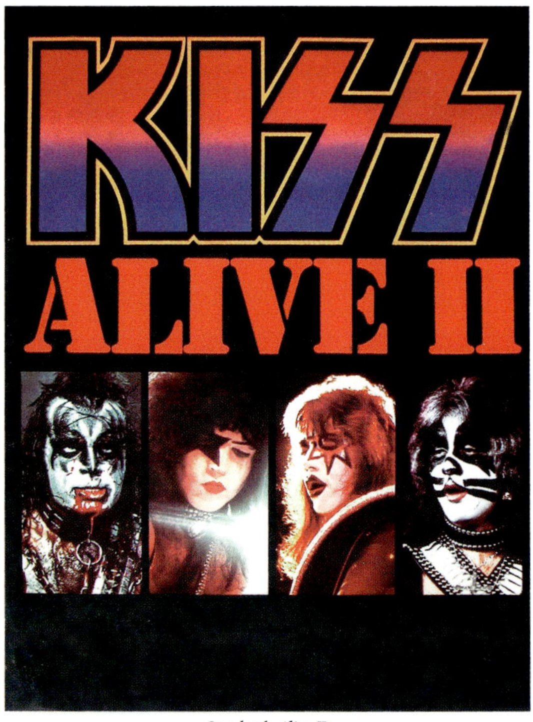

Songbook, Alive II.

Songbook, Destroyer.

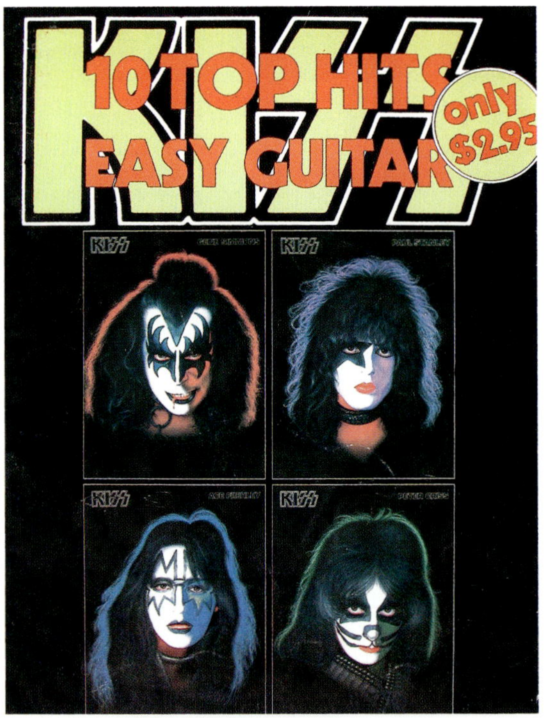

Songbook, KISS Top 10 Hits Easy Guitar.

Songbook, Love Gun.

Songbook, Rock and Roll Over.

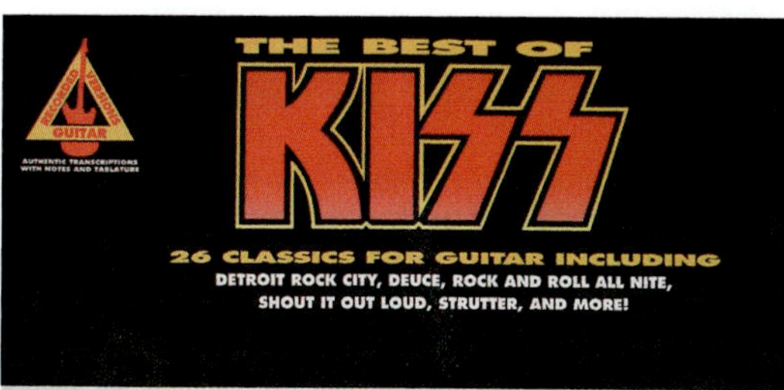

Songbook, Best of KISS.

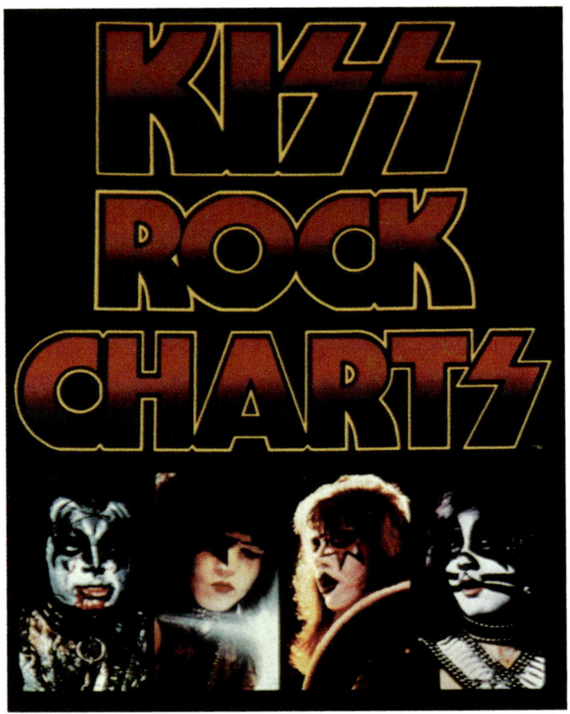

Songbook, Rock Charts. Jeff Barre collection.

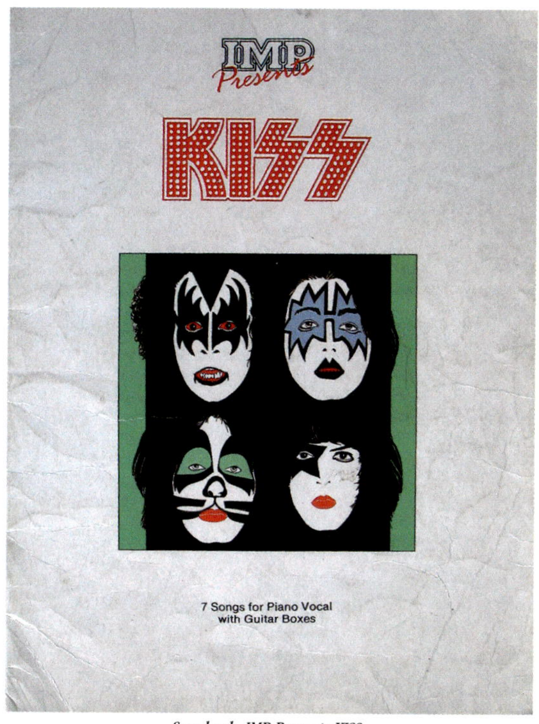

Songbook, IMP Presents KISS.

Item	VG	EX	NM
The Originals	$11-13	$23-25	$45-50
Rock and Roll Over	$6-8	$13-15	$25-30
Rock Charts w/cut-out masks	$6-8	$13-15	$25-30
The Best of KISS, skyline cover	$2-3	$4-5	$7-10
The Best of KISS, Ace cover	$5-6	$10-13	$20-25
With CD or cassette			
Unmasked	$11-13	$23-25	$45-50

Boxes, LP and cassette storage

Wooden, JC Penney exclusive			
Cassette storage, Dynasty cover	$75-88	$150-175	$300-350
LP storage, Solo faces	$75-88	$150-175	$300-350

Wooden LP storage box from JC Penney.

McFarlane mini busts, silver variant.

Item	VG	EX	NM
Busts (McFarlane)			
Full color	$1-1	$2-3	$3-5
Silver variant	$1-1	$2-3	$3-5
Busts, 20-inch			
Boxed	$15-19	$30-38	$60-75

Ace Frehley 20-inch bust.

Item	VG	EX	NM
Calendars			
Desk style			
Solo faces, 1978	$16-20	$33-40	$65-80
2002, USA	$2-3	$4-5	$7-10

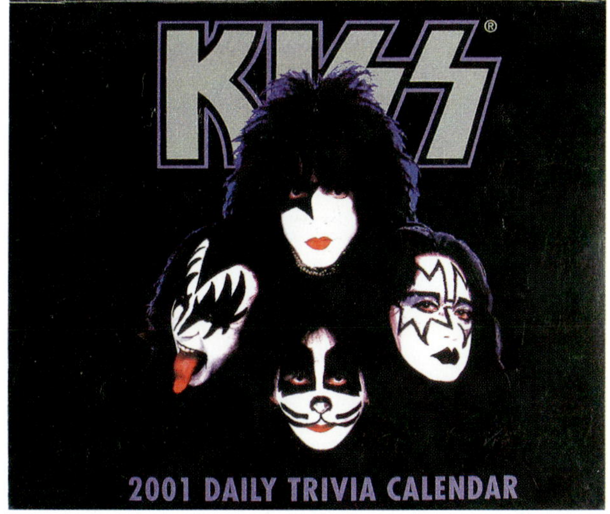

Wall trivia calendar.

A 2000 wall calendar.

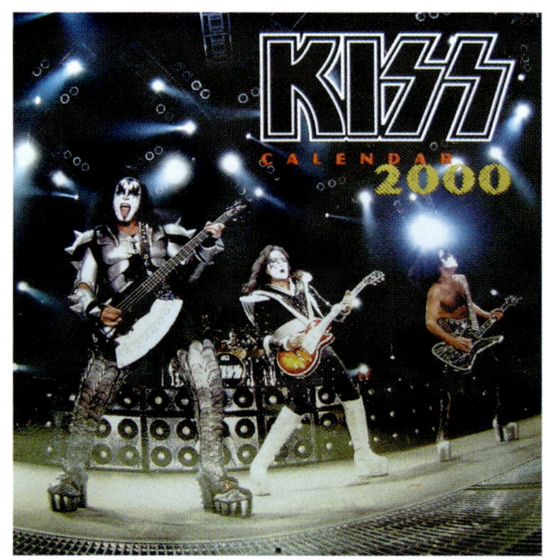

Item	VG	EX	NM
Calendars			
Wall style			
1974-1983, USA	$4-5	$8-10	$15-20
1981, Australian	$19-20	$38-40	$75-80
1984-1995, USA	$2-3	$4-5	$7-10
1996-present, USA	$1-1	$1-3	$2-5

Disposable camera.

Item	VG	EX	NM
Camera, disposable	$6-8	$13-15	$25-30

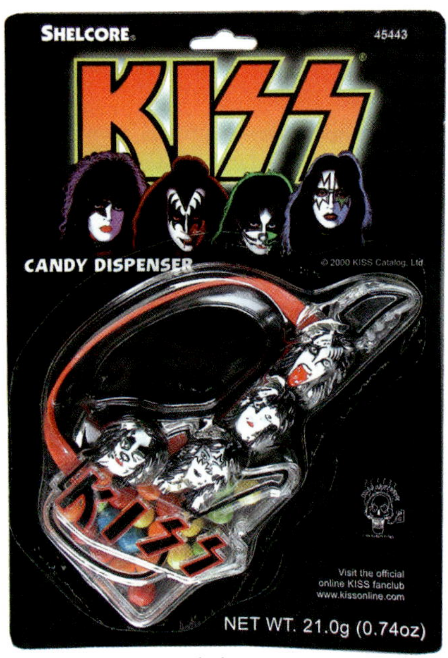

Candy dispenser.

Item	VG	EX	NM
Candy dispenser	$1-1	$1-3	$2-5

Assorted card wrappers.

Item	VG	EX	NM
Cards, collector			
(Worldwide collector cards can be seen at www.kisshall.com)			
ALIVE! (2000)			
Complete set (1-72)	$4-5	$8-10	$15-20
Binder, w/chase card S3	$4-5	$8-10	$15-20
Chase card S1	$0-0	$0-0	$0.25-0.50
Chase card S2	$0-0	$0-0	$0.25-0.50
Chase card S3	$0-0	$0-0	$0.25-0.50
Gold Record Chase card (25 total)	$2-3	$4-5	$7-10

Item	VG	EX	NM
American Images (bootleg) 1992			
Uncut sheet	$2-3	$5-6	$9-12
Complete set	$2-3	$4-5	$7-10
Single cards	$0-0	$0-0	$0.25-0.75
Cornerstone Series 1, 1997			
Complete set (1-90)	$4-5	$8-10	$15-20
Chase card, each (F1-F6)	$2-3	$4-6	$8-12
Preview Set (9 cards), sealed	$3-4	$6-8	$12-15
Promo card P1, Gene Simmons	$0-1	$1-2	$1-3
Promo card P2, Paul Stanley	$0-1	$1-2	$1-3
Promo card P3, Ace Frehley	$0-1	$1-2	$1-3
Promo card P4, Peter Criss	$0-1	$1-2	$1-3
Promo card P5, Live Shot	$2-3	$4-6	$8-12
Promo card P6, Reunion	$0-1	$1-2	$1-3
Promo card P7, First LP pose	$2-3	$4-5	$7-10
Promo card P8, Group on bars	$2-3	$4-5	$7-10
Promo card P9, Spirit Of '76	$3-4	$6-8	$12-15
Cornerstone Series 1 second print, 1998			
Complete set (1-90), red foil	$13-19	$25-38	$50-75
Complete set (1-90), gold foil	$4-5	$8-10	$15-20
Chase card, each (F1-F6)	$2-3	$4-6	$8-12
Promo card P10, Unplugged	$2-3	$4-5	$7-10
Cornerstone Series 2, 1998			
Complete set, silver foil (91-180)	$4-5	$8-10	$15-20
Complete set, blue foil (91-180)	$5-6	$10-13	$20-25
Complete set, red foil (91-180)	$13-19	$25-38	$50-75

Item	VG	EX	NM
Box topper set 9 silver foil cards	$2-3	$4-5	$8-10
Box topper set 9 blue foil cards	$2-3	$4-5	$8-10
Chase card, color border (two of each member), each	$1-1	$2-3	$3-5
Chase card, gold border (two of each member), each	$1-1	$2-3	$3-5
Promo card P1	$0-1	$1-2	$1-3
Promo card P2	$0-1	$1-2	$1-3
Promo card P3	$0-1	$1-2	$1-3
Autograph insert card (not signed)	$2-3	$4-5	$8-10
Donruss Series 1, 1978			
Complete set (1-66)	$10-16	$20-33	$40-65
Donruss Series 1 revised, 1980			
Complete set (1-66)	$31-38	$63-75	$125-150
Donruss Series 2, 1978			
Complete set (67-132)	$16-21	$33-43	$65-85
Donruss Rock Star Cards, 1978			
Complete set (1-66)	$6-10	$13-20	$25-40
Gold Collector card			
Psycho Circus	$3-4	$5-8	$10-15
Johnny Lightning			
Complete set (1-50)	$6-8	$13-15	$25-30
Card, each loose	$0-0	$0-0	$0.50-0.75
Kinetic art card (digital motion)			
Member Card	$4-5	$9-10	$17-20
Psycho Circus Tour	$4-5	$9-10	$17-20

Kinetic art card from the Psycho Circus tour.

Item	VG	EX	NM
KISS Army sign up card			
Available at 1970's concerts	$1-2	$3-4	$5-8
Monty (Holland)			
Complete set	$31-38	$63-75	$125-150
Pro Set Super Stars, 1991			
Card # 196, Asylum-era photo	$0-0	$1-1	$1-1.25
Card # 197, Dynasty-era pose	$0-0	$1-1	$1-1.25
The Originals, LP set			
Uncut from sheet	$4-6	$8-13	$15-25

A Monty card wrapper from Holland.

Item	VG	EX	NM
Web site access card			
With Eric Singer in makeup, Japan	$44-45	$88-90	$175-180

Cars and trucks, die cast

NOTE: Loose cars are worth the lowest VG price, even if NM

Item	VG	EX	NM
Action			
1/64 scale			
Kevin Harvick			
Monte Carlo (5,280)	$3-4	$6-8	$12-15
Sterling Marlin Dodge Intrepid	$1-2	$3-4	$5-8
1/43 scale			
Kevin Harvick Monster truck	$3-4	$6-8	$12-15
Johnny Lightning			
Cars			
Dragster, no letter on rear window	$2-3	$5-6	$9-12
Dragster, letter on rear window	$1-1	$1-3	$2-5
Diamond Distributor exclusive			
Dragster, purple	$2-3	$4-5	$7-10
Stock Car, black	$1-1	$1-3	$2-5
K-Mart exclusive			
Stock Car, blue	$2-3	$4-5	$7-10
Trucks			
1971 El Camino	$1-2	$2-4	$3-7
1978 Dodge	$1-2	$2-4	$3-7
Ford Model A	$1-2	$2-4	$3-7
1959 El Camino	$1-2	$2-4	$3-7

A 1/64th scale action sterling Marlin Dodge Intrepid.

Item	VG	EX	NM
1940 Ford	$1-2	$2-4	$3-7
1991 GMC Syclone	$1-2	$2-4	$3-7
White Lightning variants	$6-9	$13-18	$25-35
Racing Champions			
Hot Rockin' Steel Series			
1:64 series, members' cars			
Dodge Viper (25,000)	$1-2	$3-4	$5-8
Plymouth Prowler (9,999)	$1-2	$3-4	$5-8
1997 Mustang (9,999)	$1-2	$3-4	$5-8
Group vehicles			
KISS Prowler	$6-8	$13-15	$25-30
Prowler Club exclusive (3504)			
Psycho Circus Prowler	$5-6	$10-13	$20-25
Concert exclusive (5000)			
Silver Pro Stock Firebird	$1-2	$3-4	$5-8
Dragster (25,000)			
Red, White, and Blue			
Pro Stock Dragster	$2-3	$5-6	$9-12
Target exclusive (9,999)			
Red Corvette (9,999)	$2-3	$5-6	$9-12
1967 Chevy Chevelle (9,999)	$2-3	$5-6	$9-12
1:24 series			
#2 Silver Pro Stock Firebird Dragster (4,999)			
Boxed	$11-13	$23-25	$45-50
#5 Red, White, and Blue Pro Stock Dragster (4,999)			
Boxed	$11-13	$23-25	$45-50

A Kmart exclusive stock car, blue.

Johnny Lightning 1978 Dodge and 1971 El Camino trucks.

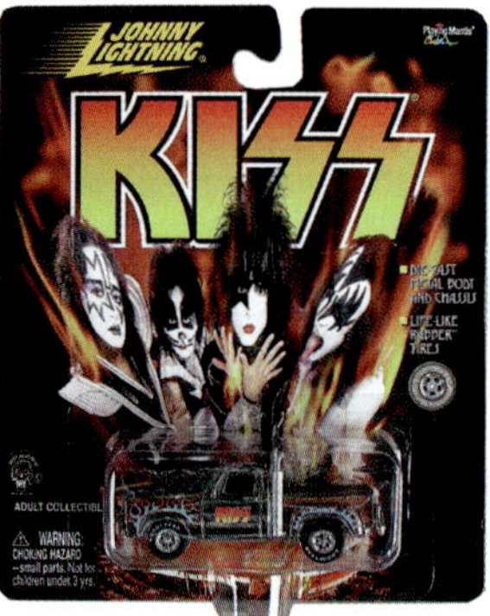

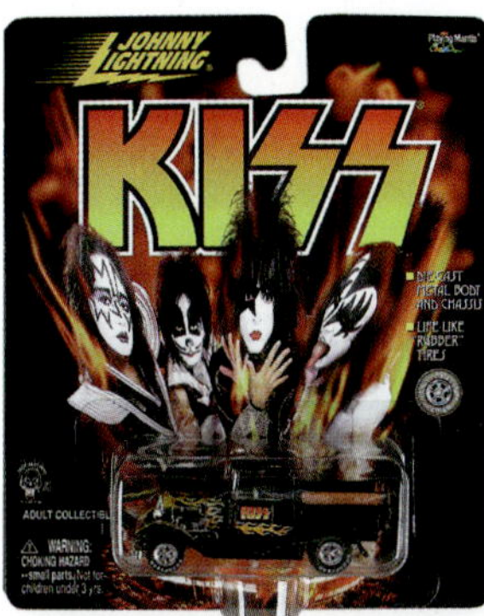

Johnny Lightning Ford Model A and 1940 Ford trucks.

Johnny Lightning 1959 El Camino and 1991 GMC Syclone trucks.

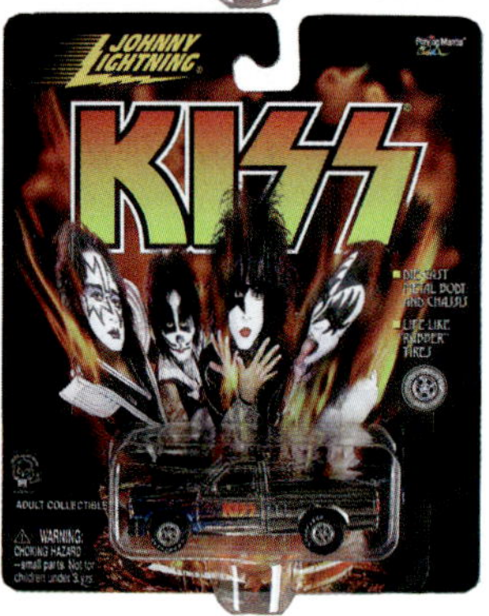

Racing Champions Mustang set.

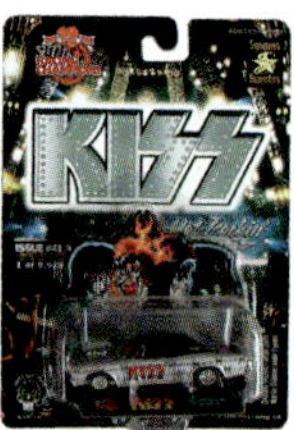

Racing Champions Chevy Chevelle barb wire cars.

Racing Champions pro stock Dragster cars.

Racing Champions pro stock Firebird cars.

Racing Champions Prowler Club exclusive.

Item	VG	EX	NM
#18 Chevy Chevelle (2,499)			
Boxed	$15-18	$30-35	$60-70
Hot Rockin' Steel Street Wheels Series			
(This series is not numbered, and is slightly smaller than 1:64 scale)			
Red Jeep	$11-13	$23-25	$45-50
Black Van	$6-8	$13-15	$25-30
Ace Frehley Mustang	$3-4	$6-8	$12-15
Peter Criss Mustang	$3-4	$6-8	$12-15
Paul Stanley Mustang	$3-4	$6-8	$12-15
Gene Simmons Mustang	$3-4	$6-8	$12-15
Five-pack (Black van and four Mustangs, one for each member)	$2-3	$5-6	$9-12

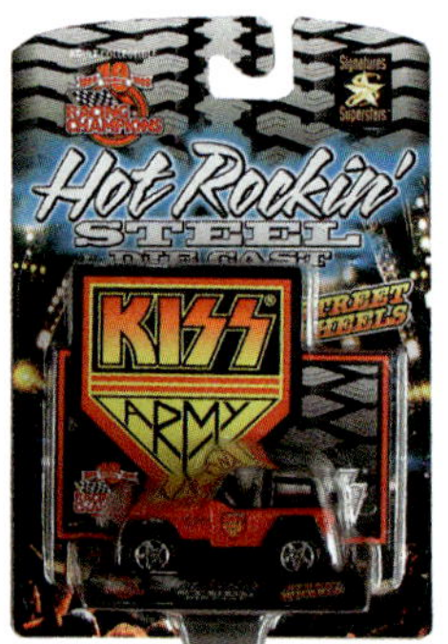

Racing Champions Street Wheels Jeep and van.

Racing Champions Hot Tracks cars.

Racing Champions Street Wheels, Hot Tracks Series five-pack.

Racing Champions Hot Tracks Series five-packs.

Item	VG	EX	NM
Hot Tracks Series			
KISS Army 1964 1/2 Mustang	$1-2	$3-4	$5-8
KISS logo 1997 Mustang	$1-2	$3-4	$5-8
Hot Tracks Series 5-pack			
NOTE: The KISS cars were never available in a one-pack by themselves			
KISS 49 Mercury and 68 Javelin, 2 NSYNC, 1 Matchbox 20	$1-2	$3-4	$5-8
KISS 79 Chevelle 69 Hurst, 1 NSYNC, 1 98, 1 Matchbox 20	$1-2	$3-4	$5-8

Item	VG	EX	NM
KISS 2 Mustangs, 1 NSYNC, 1 98, 1 Matchbox 20	$1-2	$3-4	$5-8
Casket	$200-250	$400-500	$800-1,000
CD-ROM			
KISS The Immortals	$2-3	$5-6	$9-12
KISS Pinball	$6-8	$13-15	$25-30
Nightmare Child	$4-5	$8-10	$15-20

KISS pinball available as a CD Rom and for Sony Playstation.

Nightmare Child CD Rom game, collectors' edition.

Inflatable chair. Rich Vanderwerken collection.

Item	VG	EX	NM
Chair, inflatable			
Solo faces with cup holder			
Boxed	$13-19	$25-38	$50-75

Item	VG	EX	NM
Christmas ornaments, ball style			
Destroyer, boxed	$2-2	$3-5	$6-9
Hand Painted Faces, boxed	$5-8	$10-15	$20-30
Rock and Roll Over, boxed	$2-2	$3-5	$6-9
The following have a black KISS logo on back			
Psycho Circus, boxed	$2-2	$3-5	$6-9
Rock and Roll Over, boxed	$2-2	$3-5	$6-9
Saw Blade Logo, boxed	$2-2	$3-5	$6-9
Worldwide Convention, boxed	$2-2	$3-5	$6-9
Clocks			
3-D with Ax pendulum	$9-10	$18-20	$35-40
Group pose, wall style	$9-11	$18-23	$35-45
Destroyer, 12" wall style	$6-8	$13-15	$25-30
KISS Army, 3" flip clock	$9-10	$18-20	$35-40
Live, wall style	$9-11	$18-23	$35-45
Psycho Circus Cover CD	$3-4	$6-8	$12-15
Rock And Roll Over, wall style	$4-5	$9-10	$17-20
Solo faces, wall style	$4-5	$9-10	$17-20
Spinning pedestal, KISS Army	$9-11	$18-23	$35-45
Coins, sets			
Liberty Mint			
Alive/Worldwide 1996-97, silver (2,500)			
Each member sealed on card	$3-4	$6-8	$12-15
Set of four in case	$30-33	$60-65	$120-130

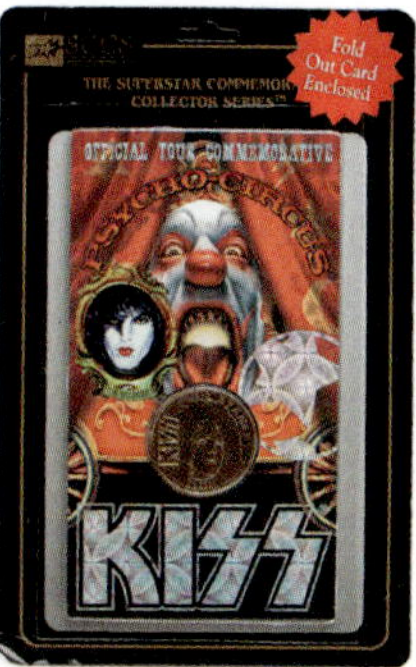

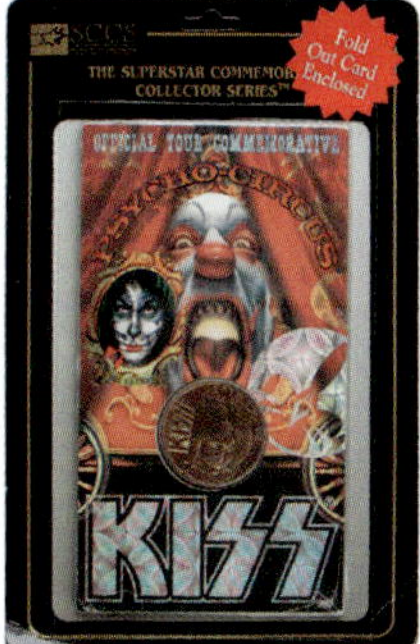

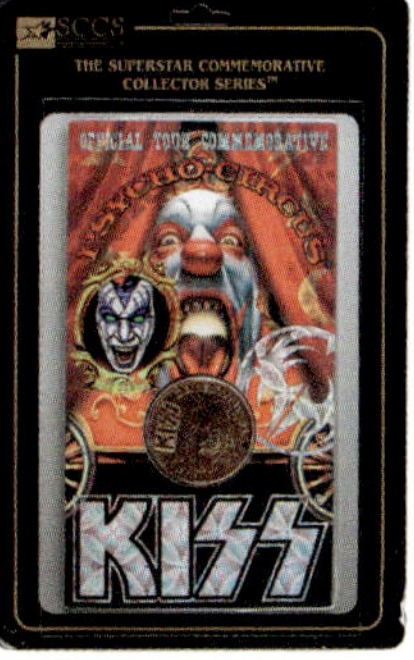

Psycho Circus tour commemorative coins.

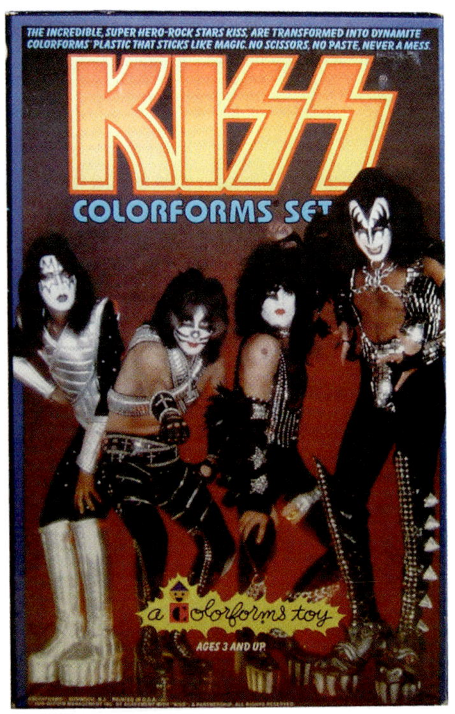
THE INCREDIBLE, SUPER HERO-ROCK STARS KISS, ARE TRANSFORMED INTO DYNAMITE
COLORFORMS PLASTIC THAT STICKS LIKE MAGIC. NO SCISSORS, NO PASTE, NEVER A MESS.
KISS
COLORFORMS SET
a Colorforms toy
AGES 3 AND UP

Colorforms.

Item	VG	EX	NM
Alive/Worldwide 1996-97, gold (1,000)			
Each member sealed on card	$11-14	$23-28	$45-55
Set of four in case	$50-55	$100-110	$200-220
Psycho Circus, silver			
Each member sealed on card	$6-8	$13-15	$25-30
Set of four in case	$31-35	$63-70	$125-140
Psycho Circus, gold-plated			
Each member sealed on card	$3-4	$6-9	$12-17
Set of four in case	$15-20	$30-40	$60-80

Item	VG	EX	NM
Colorforms	$44-50	$88-100	$175-200

Comics

Item	VG	EX	NM
Animaniacs #16	$0-1	$1-2	$1-3
Green Lantern MOSAIC [Revenge ad on back]	$1-1	$1-3	$2-5
Dark Horse Comics #1	$0-1	$1-2	$1-3
Howard the Duck #12	$1-1	$1-3	$2-5
Howard the Duck #13	$1-1	$1-3	$2-5
Marvel Comic #1	$25-31	$50-63	$100-125
Marvel Comic #2	$9-11	$18-23	$35-45
Marvel KISS Classics	$2-3	$4-5	$7-10
Marvel KISS Nation	$4-5	$8-10	$15-20
Psycho Circus #1, 1st print only	$2-3	$4-5	$7-10
Psycho Circus #2 to present	$0-1	$1-2	$1-3
Rock And Roll Comics	$1-1	$1-3	$2-5
Spider-Man Team-Up #5	$0-1	$1-2	$1-3
Tales From The Tours	$1-1	$1-3	$2-5

Marvel KISS Comic Number 1.

Marvel KISS Comic Number 2.

Dark Horse Comics Issue Number 1 with autograph band and guitar picks.

Dark Horse Comics Issue Number 1 pre-production sheets.

Item	VG	EX	NM
Condoms			
Black pack	$4-5	$8-10	$15-20
KISS Kondoms			
Love Gun Protection, single	$0-0	$0-1	$0.75-1
Studded Paul, single	$0-0	$0-1	$0.75-1
Tongue Lubricated, single	$0-0	$0-1	$0.75-1
Box	$1-1	$1-3	$2-5
Display stand	$4-5	$8-10	$15-20
Display jar	$4-5	$8-10	$15-20
Key chain condom	$4-5	$8-10	$15-20
Konfidential (promo)	$4-5	$8-10	$15-20
Rise To It	$4-5	$8-10	$15-20
Unholy	$4-5	$8-10	$15-20
White pack	$4-5	$8-10	$15-20

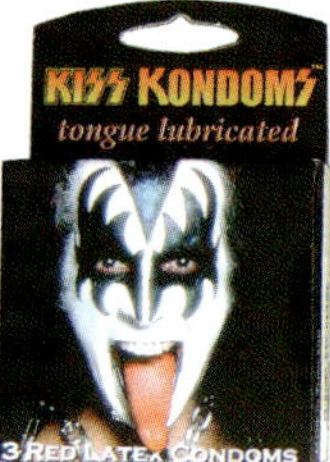

Tongue Lubricated, Love Gun Protection, and Studded Paul condoms.

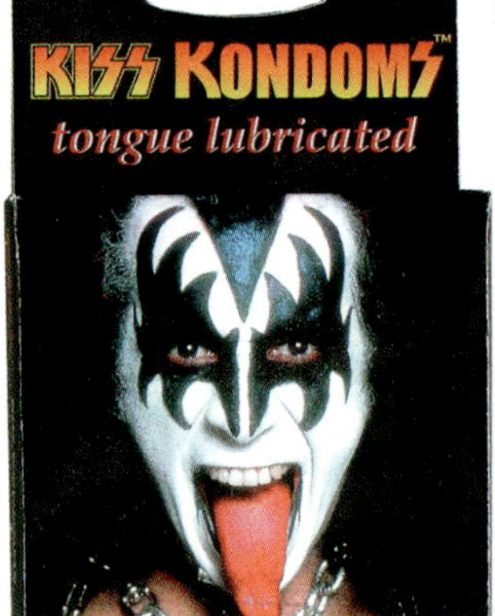

Tongue Lubricated condoms box and pack.

Assorted credit cards. No value in book because no one trades these.

Item	VG	EX	NM
Cups, plastic			
Magic Market Cups, each	$10-14	$20-28	$40-55
Spin Magazine stadium cup	$1-3	$3-5	$5-10
Superdome stadium cup, 1996, not official	$1-1	$2-3	$3-5
Doormats			
KISS Army	$6-8	$13-15	$25-30
KISS Icons	$6-8	$13-15	$25-30
Solo LPs, Casablanca (promo)	$38-50	$75-100	$150-200

Drumsticks

(Links to see all KISS drumsticks can be found at www.kisshall.com)

Note: Values are for an individual stick, not pairs.

Peter Criss

Alive/Destroyer tours

Item	VG	EX	NM
Cappella - cobalt blue/natural oak wood, professional percussion	$50-56	$100-113	$200-225
Rock and Roll Over/Love Gun tours			
Cappella - cobalt blue/natural oak wood, pro percussion	$44-50	$88-100	$175-200
Cappella - light metallic blue/natural oak wood, pro percussion	$19-25	$38-50	$75-100

Magic Market cups. Rich Vanderwerken collection.

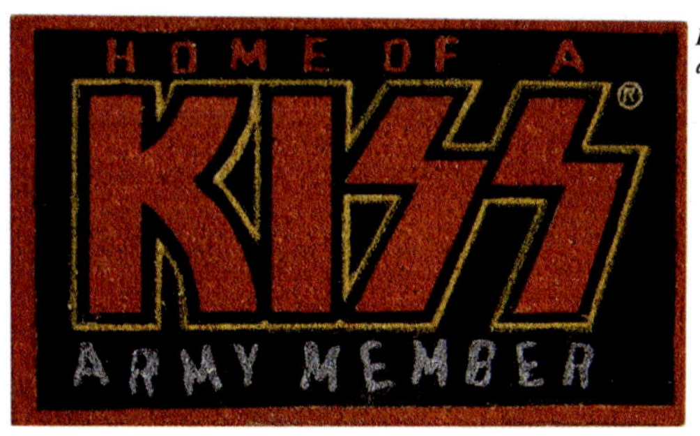

KISS Army doormat.

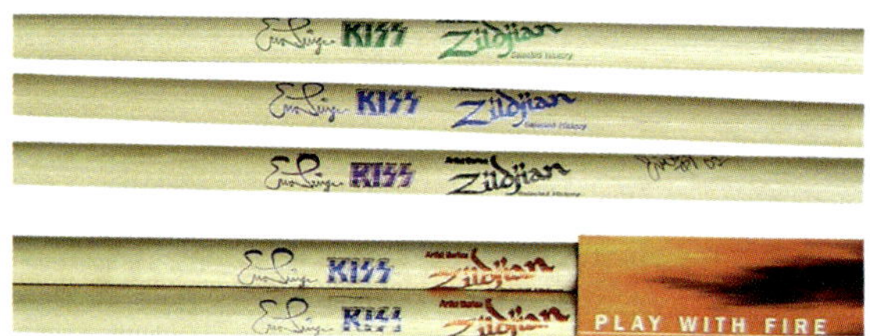

Eric Singer makeup-era drumsticks.

Item	VG	EX	NM
Alive II Tour			
Calato Regal Tip 5B – black/natural wood	$25-31	$50-63	$100-125
Farewell Tour			
Easton Ahead 5B - white/black w/drum tattoo and KISS logo, concert model, studio model, and PC3 model	$6-8	$13-15	$25-30
World Domination Tour			
Generic Zildjian Jazz Model	$8-19	$15-38	$30-75
Eric Carr			
Creatures tour			
Calato Regal Tip 2B - black/natural wood – KISS logo/signature	$38-44	$75-88	$150-175
Rug Caddy 2B - silver/natural wood, outlined KISS logo/ERIC CARR printed	$13-19	$25-38	$50-75

Item	VG	EX	NM
Lick It Up tour			
ProMark Oak 5B - brown/natural wood, ERIC CARR-KISS printed	$31-38	$63-75	$125-150
Rug Caddy 2B - black/natural wood, outlined KISS logo/ERIC CARR printed	$13-19	$25-38	$50-75
Cappella - cobalt blue/natural oak wood, ERIC CARR-KISS printed	$25-31	$50-63	$100-125
Eric Singer			
(All Eric Singer sticks have his signature on the graphics; KISS logo is outlined unless noted)			
Revenge club tour			
Zildjian - black/hickory, KISS and Zildjian logos	$31-38	$63-75	$125-150
Zildjian - red/hickory, KISS and Zildjian logos	$25-31	$50-63	$100-125
Farewell Tour			
Zildjian - metallic green/hickory, KISS and Artist Series logos	$11-13	$23-25	$45-50
Zildjian - metallic blue/hickory, KISS and Artist Series logos	$11-13	$23-25	$45-50
Zildjian - purple and black/hickory, KISS and Artist Series logos	$3-4	$5-8	$10-15

Fireman's helmets

Item	VG	EX	NM
Logo and number 3	$200-300	$400-600	$800-1,200

Item	VG	EX	NM
Logo and signature			
Red	$200-300	$400-600	$800-1,200
Yellow	$200-300	$400-600	$800-1,200
White	$200-300	$400-600	$800-1,200
Black	$200-300	$400-600	$800-1,200
No custom badge	$13-15	$25-30	$50-60

Games

Item	VG	EX	NM
On Tour, 1978	$56-63	$113-125	$225-250
KISSopoly	$5-6	$10-13	$20-25
KISS Trivia	$3-4	$6-8	$12-15

Glassware

Item	VG	EX	NM
Silver drinking glass	$2-3	$4-5	$7-10
Beer stein			
White			
Black logo w/first LP photo	$4-5	$8-10	$15-20
Red logo	$4-5	$8-10	$15-20
Pewter, with member on lid, boxed	$44-50	$88-100	$175-200
Chalice			
KISS Army	$4-5	$8-10	$15-20
Psycho Circus	$4-5	$8-10	$15-20
Ceramic head mug			
Any member	$2-3	$4-5	$7-10
Coffee mug			
Black, red logo	$2-3	$4-5	$7-10

KISS Trivia Game.

Silver drinking glass.

Gene Simmons ceramic head mug.

Item	VG	EX	NM
Clear			
Black logo w/first LP photo	$2-3	$4-5	$7-10
Red logo	$2-3	$4-5	$7-10
White			
Black logo w/first LP photo	$5-6	$10-13	$20-25
Red logo	$2-3	$4-5	$7-10
Reunion photo, purple	$2-3	$4-5	$7-10
Reunion photo, red	$2-3	$4-5	$7-10
Shooter glasses			
Set of two	$4-5	$8-9	$15-18
Reunion faces	$2-3	$4-5	$7-10
Solo Faces	$2-3	$4-5	$7-10

Clear tankard.

Far right, shooter glass, Reunion faces; shot glass, Psycho Circus comic faces.

Item	VG	EX	NM
Shot glasses	$1-2	$3-4	$5-8
Tankard, clear			
Black logo w/first LP photo	$2-3	$5-6	$9-12
Psycho Circus	$8-9	$15-18	$30-35
Red logo	$2-3	$5-6	$9-12
All Four faces	$3-4	$6-8	$12-15
Glitter lamp	$10-13	$20-25	$40-50
Golf equipment			
Golf balls			
Note: Deduct 50%, if not boxed			
KISS Army, three-pack	$1-1	$2-3	$3-5
KISS Army, six-pack	$3-4	$6-8	$12-15
Rock and Roll Over, three-pack	$1-1	$2-3	$3-5
Rock and Roll Over, six-pack	$3-4	$6-8	$12-15
Divot tool			
KISS Army, three-pack	$3-4	$6-8	$12-15
Rock and Roll Over, three-pack	$3-4	$6-8	$12-15
Gloves			
KISS Army	$3-4	$6-8	$12-15
Rock and Roll Over	$3-4	$6-8	$12-15
Gruntz			
Hotter Than Hell	$2-3	$4-5	$7-10
Dressed To Kill	$2-3	$4-5	$7-10

Glitter lamp.

Three-pack of golf balls, Rock and Roll Over.

KISS
ACE FREHLEY
WARNING:
CHOKING HAZARD
KISS
PAUL STANLEY
WARNING:
CHOKING HAZARD
KISS
PETER CRISS
WARNING:
CHOKING HAZARD
KISS
GENE SIMMONS
WARNING:
CHOKING HAZARD

Gruntz.

Item	VG	EX	NM

Guitars and equipment, member endorsed

Ace Frehley

Item	VG	EX	NM
Epiphone, Ace Frehley/Les Paul	$125-150	$250-300	$500-600
Gibson, Ace Frehley/Les Paul, Custom (300)	$1,250-1375	$2,500-2,750	$5,000-5,500
Gibson, Ace Frehley/Les Paul	$625-750	$1,250-1,500	$2,500-3,000
Washburn AF-40V	$500-625	$1,000-1,250	$2,000-2,500
Washburn AF-40V, signed (300)	$450-500	$900-1,000	$1,800-2,000

Paul Stanley

Item	VG	EX	NM
Ibanez PS-10, 1979	$375-500	$750-1,000	$1,500-2,000
Ibanez PS-10 Ltd., 1995 (300)	$450-550	$900-1,100	$1,800-2,200
Ibanez PS-10 Classic, 1996	$375-500	$750-1,000	$1,500-2,000
Randall Colossus amp	$125-150	$250-300	$500-600
Silvertone Warm Up Amp	$13-14	$25-28	$50-55
Silvertone Apocalypse Pro	$100-108	$200-215	$400-430
Silvertone Apocalypse Special	$56-63	$113-125	$225-250
Silvertone Apocalypse Bass	$56-63	$113-125	$225-250
Silvertone Dark Star Acoustic	$44-45	$88-90	$175-180
Silvertone Sovereign Pro	$100-108	$200-215	$400-430
Silvertone Sovereign Special	$50-54	$100-108	$200-215
Washburn PS2000B	$500-625	$1,000-1,250	$2,000-2,500
Washburn PS2000M	$1,250-1,375	$2,000-2,750	$5,000-5,500
Washburn PS500B	$100-125	$200-250	$400-500
Washburn PS100B	$125-150	$250-300	$500-600
Washburn PS2000 Millennium	$1,250-1,375	$2,500-2,750	$5,000-5,500
Washburn PS2000 Rose	$500-625	$1,000-1,250	$2,000-2,500

Ace Frehley Epiphone guitars, courtesy Gibson Guitars.

Ace Frehley Epiphone Headstock close up.

Item	VG	EX	NM
Gene Simmons			
Ax bass, 1998	$450-500	$900-1,000	$1,800-2,000
Ax bass, Kramer, 1978	$625-750	$1,250-1,500	$2,500-3,000
Punisher bass	$225-250	$450-500	$900-1,000
Punisher bass head	$113-125	$225-250	$450-500

Ace Frehley Gibson custom shop model, courtesy Gibson Guitars.

A rare blue body variation of the Ace Frebley Gibson custom 300 guitar. Courtesy Gibson Guitars.

Paul Stanley Randall Colossus amp.

Paul Stanley signature model PS2000B, courtesy Washburn Guitars.

Paul Stanley signature model PS500B, courtesy Washburn Guitars.

Paul Stanley signature model PS100B, courtesy Washburn Guitars.

Paul Stanley signature model PS2000M, courtesy Washburn Guitars.

Paul Stanley signature model PS2000 Millennium, courtesy Washburn Guitars.

Paul Stanley signature model PS2000 Washburn Rose, courtesy Washburn Guitars.

Paul Stanley signature model PS2000FL, a color variation of PS2000B (same pricing), courtesy Washburn Guitars.

Paul Stanley signature model PS2000SS, a color variation of PS2000B (same pricing), courtesy Washburn Guitars.

Item	VG	EX	NM
Guitar picks			
(Photos of all KISS picks can be seen at www.kisshall.com)			
Pre-Rock and Roll Over			
Ace Frehley and Paul Stanley			
Black print on white pick, printed name on one side w/PASTORE MUSIC on the back	$125-150	$250-300	$500-600
Gene Simmons			
Black print on white pick, printed $immons on one side w/a blank back	$81-88	$163-175	$325-350
Rock and Roll Over			
Black print on bone picks, printed name on one side with a tall solid logo on the other.			
Ace Frehley and Paul Stanley	$50-63	$100-120	$200-250
Gene Simmons	$63-69	$125-138	$250-275
Love Gun/Alive II Tours			
Black print on bone picks, signature on one side with a tall solid logo on the other.			
Ace Frehley, Paul Stanley and Gene Simmons	$25-31	$50-63	$100-125
Dynasty Tour			
Black print on bone picks, Dynasty signature on one side with an outlined logo on the other.			
Ace Frehley	$13-19	$25-38	$50-75
Paul Stanley	$13-19	$25-38	$50-75
Gene Simmons	$13-19	$25-38	$50-75

Item	VG	EX	NM
Unmasked Tour			
Silver print on semi transparent white picks, Dynasty signature on one side, with an outlined logo on the other.			
Ace Frehley	$6-19	$33-38	$65-75
Paul Stanley and Gene Simmons	$9-13	$18-25	$35-50
Creatures of the Night Tour			
Silver print on white picks, Dynasty signature on one side with an outlined logo on the other.			
Ace Frehley	$6-19	$33-38	$65-75
Paul Stanley and Gene Simmons	$9-13	$18-25	$35-50
Vinnie Vincent, one-line sig	$19-25	$38-50	$75-100
Silver print on white picks, Love Gun signature on one side with a tall logo on the other.			
Paul Stanley and Gene Simmons	$75-88	$150-175	$300-350
Vinnie Vincent	$88-100	$175-200	$350-400
Black print on white picks, Love Gun signature on one side with a tall logo on the other.			
Paul Stanley, Gene Simmons and Vinnie Vincent	$25-31	$50-63	$100-125
Lick It Up Tour			
Black print on white picks, Love Gun signature on one side with a tall logo on the other.			
Paul Stanley, Gene Simmons and Vinnie Vincent	$25-31	$50-63	$100-125
Black print on yellow picks, Love Gun signature on one side with an outlined logo on the other.			
Paul Stanley and Gene Simmons	$6-10	$13-20	$25-40

Rock Over Tour guitar picks. Jeff Stouder collection.

Item	VG	EX	NM
Vinnie Vincent, two-line sig	$13-16	$25-33	$50-65

Animalize Tour

Black print on semi-transparent white picks (except Paul's), Love Gun signature on one side with an outlined logo on the other.

Paul Stanley and Gene Simmons	$6-10	$13-20	$25-40

Black print on semi-transparent white picks, blank on one side with an outlined logo on the other.

Mark St. John and Bruce Kulick	$6-10	$13-20	$25-40

Gold print on semi-transparent white picks (except Paul's), Love Gun signature on one side with an outlined logo on the other.

Paul Stanley and Gene Simmons	$6-10	$13-20	$25-40

Gold print on semi transparent white picks, blank on one side with an outlined logo on the other.

Mark St. John and Bruce Kulick	$6-10	$13-20	$25-40

Asylum Tour

Gold print on brown picks, signature on one side with an outlined logo on the other.

Paul Stanley, Gene Simmons and Bruce Kulick	$75-88	$150-175	$300-350

Dynasty Tour guitar picks. Jeff Stouder collection.

Item	VG	EX	NM
Gold print on blue picks, signature on one side with an outlined logo on the other.			
Paul Stanley	$38-44	$75-88	$150-175
Gene Simmons	$13-19	$25-38	$50-75
Bruce Kuick	$8-10	$15-20	$30-40
Gold print on pink picks, signature on one side with an outlined logo on the other.			
Gold print on red picks, signature on one side with an outlined logo on the other.			
Powder gold print on yellow picks, signature on one side with an outlined logo on the other.			
Paul Stanley	$21-25	$43-50	$85-100
Gene Simmons	$13-19	$25-38	$50-75
Bruce Kulick	$8-10	$15-20	$30-40
Powder gold print on white picks, signature on one side with an outlined logo on the other.			
Paul Stanley, Gene Simmons and Bruce Kulick	$8-10	$15-20	$30-40

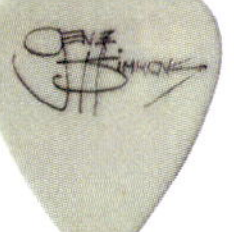

Creatures Tour tall silver logo guitar picks. Jeff Stouder collection.

Creatures Tour tall black logo guitar picks. Jeff Stouder collection.

Item	VG	EX	NM
Crazy Nights			
Gold print on white picks, signature on one side with an outlined logo on the other.			
Paul Stanley, Gene Simmons and Bruce Kulick	$3-5	$5-10	$10-20
Silver print on white picks, signature on one side with an outlined logo on the other.			
Paul Stanley, Gene Simmons and Bruce Kulick	$19-21	$38-43	$75-85
Paul Stanley Solo Tour			
Gold print on white picks, Love Gun signature on one side with the other blank.			
Paul Stanley	$4-8	$8-15	$15-30

Item	VG	EX	NM
Hot in the Shade Tour			
These picks are identical to the Crazy Nights tour gold on white picks			
Gold print on white picks, signature on one side with an outlined logo on the other.			
Paul Stanley, Gene Simmons and Bruce Kulick	$3-5	$5-10	$10-20
Revenge Club Tour			
Black print on milky white picks, signature on one side with an outlined logo on the other.			
Paul Stanley, Gene Simmons and Bruce Kulick	$5-6	$10-13	$20-25
Revenge Arena Tour			
Gold print on white and off-white picks, signature on one side with an outlined logo on the other.			
Paul Stanley, Gene Simmons and Bruce Kulick	$3-5	$5-10	$10-20
Black print on yellow picks, signature on one side with an outlined logo on the other.			
Bruce Kulick	$3-5	$5-10	$10-20

Crazy Nights Tour guitar picks. Jeff Stouder and Ken Rodenas collections.

Item	VG	EX	NM
ESP pick for NAMM convention			
Black print on white picks, one-line signature and a KISS logo on one side with an ESP logo on the other.			
White print on black picks, one-line signature and a KISS logo on one side with an ESP logo on the other.			
Bruce Kulick	$3-4	$6-8	$12-15
Black print on white picks, one-line signature and a KISS logo on one side, ESP logo in a box on the other.			
White print on black picks, one-line signature and a KISS logo on one side, ESP logo in a box on the other.			
Bruce Kulick	$5-6	$10-13	$20-25
Alive/Worldwide 1996-1997 Tour			
There are many variations of this pick set. See them all at www.kisshall.com			
Ace Frehley			
Black print on glow	$5-6	$10-13	$20-25
Black print on white	$6-8	$13-15	$25-30
Blue print on glow	$5-6	$10-13	$20-25
Hologram print on black			
Fractured Prism	$5-6	$10-13	$20-25
Block prism	$10-13	$20-25	$40-50
Hologram print on clear orange	$38-44	$75-88	$150-175
Hologram print on clear blue			
Fractured prism	$4-5	$8-9	$15-18
Block prism	$6-8	$13-15	$25-30
Hologram print on clear red	$4-5	$8-9	$15-18
Hologram print on pink	$5-6	$10-13	$20-25

Ace Frehely Gibson guitar picks. Jeff Stouder collection.

Item	VG	EX	NM
Fractured prism	$5-6	$10-13	$20-25
Block and large dot prisms	$6-8	$13-15	$25-30
Hologram print on white	$4-5	$8-9	$15-18
Hologram print on white. KISS logo only, no tour logo. This was a rehearsal pick that has a different hologram pattern than the later Farewell tour fractured pick.			
Fractured prism	$38-50	$75-100	$150-200
Peter Criss			
White print on powder green	$4-5	$8-9	$15-18
Paul Stanley			
Black print on white	$4-5	$8-9	$15-18
Hologram print on black			
Fractured prism	$4-5	$8-9	$15-18
Block prism	$5-6	$10-13	$20-25
Purple print on glow	$5-6	$10-13	$20-25
Gene Simmons			
Hologram print on white	$38-44	$75-88	$150-175
Black print on white	$4-5	$8-9	$15-18
Black print on off white	$5-6	$10-13	$20-25

Paul Stanley Washburn guitar picks.

Item	VG	EX	NM
Alive/Worldwide 1996-1997 promo phone card picks			
Phone card picks have the Alive/Worldwide 96-97 tour name on the logo side, with no dash between the 96 and 97. There are many variations of this pick set. See them all at www.kisshall.com			
Ace, Peter, Paul and Gene	$2-3	$4-5	$7-10
Psycho Circus Tour			
There are many variations of this pick set. See them all at www.kisshall.com			
Ace Frehley			
Hologram print on white	$4-5	$8-9	$15-18
Hologram print on clear blue			
Dot and interlocking circle prisms	$4-5	$8-9	$15-18
Camouflage prism	$5-6	$10-13	$20-25
Paul Stanley			
Black print on white	$13-15	$25-30	$50-60
Hologram print on white	$4-5	$8-9	$15-18
Gene Simmons, black print on white	$4-5	$8-9	$15-18
Peter Criss, white print on green	$4-5	$8-9	$15-18

Item	VG	EX	NM
Psycho Circus, retail sale only			
Ace Frehley			
Sealed pack of two picks on card	$3-4	$6-8	$12-15
Photo with two picks in frame	$2-3	$4-5	$7-10
Loose, each pick	$0-1	$1-2	$1-4

Farewell Tour

Farewell tour picks have an outlined KISS logo on one side.

There are *many* variations of this pick set. See them all at www.kisshall.com

Item	VG	EX	NM
Ace Frehley			
Black print on white	$3-4	$6-8	$12-15
Black print on white, big logo	$5-6	$10-13	$20-25
Hologram print on clear blue	$3-4	$6-8	$12-15
Fractured prism	$8-10	$15-20	$30-40
Bubble and confetti prisms	$3-4	$6-8	$12-15
Hologram print on white	$3-4	$6-8	$12-15
Fractured prism	$8-10	$15-20	$30-40
Bubble and confetti prisms	$3-4	$6-8	$12-15
Ace Frehley City Picks			
North Charleston SC	$6-8	$13-15	$25-30
Gold Coast Australia	$6-8	$13-15	$25-30
All others	$3-4	$6-8	$12-15
Paul Stanley			
Black print on glossy white	$3-4	$6-8	$12-15
With Reunion tour signature (used on the movie shoot for Detroit Rock City).			
Black print on white	$6-8	$13-15	$25-30

Item	VG	EX	NM
Peter Criss			
White on clear green	$3-4	$6-8	$12-15
White on solid dark green	$3-4	$6-8	$12-15
With flip off hand on signature side of pick			
White on solid dark green	$2-2	$3-4	$6-8
Farewell 2000 under logo, white on green	$5-5	$9-10	$18-20
Gene Simmons, black print on white	$2-3	$5-6	$9-12
Eric Singer			
Japan 2001 over the KISS logo			
Dark green on black, silver logo	$5-6	$10-13	$20-25
All others	$2-3	$5-6	$9-12
Australia 2001 over the KISS logo			
Blue print on white	$4-5	$8-9	$15-18
Silver on black	$2-3	$5-6	$9-12

World Domination Tour

World Domination tour picks have an outlined KISS logo on one side

Item	VG	EX	NM
Paul Stanley			
Black print on semitransparent			
White	$2-3	$5-6	$9-12
Silver print on white	$2-3	$5-6	$9-12
Peter Criss			
White on clear green	$2-3	$5-6	$9-12
Red and white on green, PeterCriss.net on logo side	$2-3	$5-6	$9-12
Gene Simmons			
Black print on white	$2-3	$5-6	$9-12

Item	VG	EX	NM
Same as Farewell tour pick			
Tommy Thayer			
Black print on white	$2-3	$4-5	$7-10

Rock the Nation Tour

World Domination tour picks have an outlined KISS logo on one side.

Item	VG	EX	NM
Paul Stanley			
Silver print on black	$8-10	$15-20	$30-40
Silver print on white	$2-3	$5-6	$9-12
Flag print on white	$25-31	$50-63	$100-125
Gene Simmons			
Black print on white	$2-3	$5-6	$9-12
Same as Farewell tour pick			
Tommy Thayer			
Black print on white	$2-3	$4-5	$7-10
White print on black	$2-3	$4-5	$7-10
Eric Singer, silver print on black	$2-3	$5-6	$9-12

2005 Rockin' the Corps

This one off show was a benefit performed for military personnel only. KISS performed a short set. Only Paul Stanley had a custom pick for the show.

Item	VG	EX	NM
Paul Stanley, green camouflage print on white	$25-31	$50-63	$100-125

Item	VG	EX	NM
Guitar pickups (mini guitar)			
Ace Frehley, Gibson	$2-3	$4-5	$7-10
Ace Frehley, Gibson, autographed	$20-25	$40-50	$80-100
Guitar strap, strings, picks			
Ace Frehley, Gibson Master pack	$11-13	$23-25	$45-50
Guitar/toy			
Sealed	$325-375	$650-750	$1,300-1,500
Loose	$63-75	$125-150	$250-300
Backing board only	$9-10	$18-20	$35-40
Halloween costumes			
Collegeville, 1978, each member			
Boxed	$38-43	$75-85	$150-170
Loose	$11-14	$23-28	$45-55
Mask only	$4-5	$8-10	$15-20
Halloween helmet mask			
Each member	$5-6	$10-13	$20-25

Pickups mini Ace Frehley Gibson guitar.

Ace Frehely Gibson guitar master pack of string, strap and picks.

A 1970's toy guitar. Rich Vanderwerken collection.

Item	VG	EX	NM
Hats			
Baseball style			
Brown corduroy with logo	$1-2	$3-4	$5-8
Camouflage with logo	$3-4	$6-8	$12-15
Flames with logo and number 2	$6-8	$13-15	$25-30
Green corduroy with logo	$4-5	$8-10	$15-20
KISS Army, olive green	$4-5	$8-10	$15-20
Alive/Worldwide tour back	$4-5	$8-10	$15-20
Farewell Tour back	$4-5	$8-10	$15-20
Bucket style	$4-5	$8-10	$15-20
Driver's style, black	$1-2	$3-4	$5-7
Knit cap style			
Beanie black with icons	$4-5	$8-10	$15-20
Beanie gray with orange logo	$4-5	$8-10	$15-20
KISS Army	$3-4	$6-8	$12-15
Psycho Circus logo			
Brown	$3-4	$6-8	$12-15
Maroon and Black	$3-4	$6-8	$12-15
Solo faces	$3-4	$6-8	$12-15
Headliners (mini big head figurines)			
Each member			
Destroyer outfit			
Boxed	$3-4	$6-8	$12-15
Destroyer outfit, Spencer Gifts' exclusive			
Boxed	$3-4	$6-8	$12-15

Headliners, Destroyer outfit.

Incense sticks.

Item	VG	EX	NM
Love Gun outfit			
Boxed	$3-4	$6-8	$12-15

Incense sticks

Packs of sticks	$1-1	$1-3	$2-5

Incense burner

Resin, sculpted heads	$5-6	$10-13	$20-25
KISS Army, wooden	$1-2	$2-3	$3-6
Psycho Circus, wooden	$1-2	$2-3	$3-6
Skull cross, metal	$3-4	$6-8	$12-15

Ink pens. Rich Vanderwerken collection.

Item	VG	EX	NM
Ink pen			
Ace Frehley			
Sealed	$25-31	$50-63	$100-125
Loose	$13-16	$25-33	$50-65
Peter Criss			
Sealed	$69-75	$138-150	$275-300
Loose	$25-28	$50-55	$100-110

Item	VG	EX	NM
Paul Stanley			
Sealed	$23-25	$45-50	$90-100
Loose	$13-16	$25-33	$50-65
Gene Simmons			
Sealed	$20-23	$40-45	$80-90
Loose	$13-16	$25-33	$50-65

Jersey

Item	VG	EX	NM
Hockey			
KISS Army	$13-15	$25-30	$50-60
Rock and Roll Over	$13-15	$25-30	$50-60
Football			
Each Member	$11-13	$23-25	$45-50
Baseball (bootleg)			
Each member	$9-10	$18-20	$35-40

Jewelry

Item	VG	EX	NM
Bracelets			
Logo band, brass	$4-5	$8-10	$15-20
Logo band, sterling silver, 7-1/2"	$11-13	$23-25	$45-50
Logo ID bracelet, sterling silver, 7"	$11-13	$23-25	$45-50
Logo ID bracelet, sterling silver, 8"	$16-18	$33-35	$65-70
Logo, gold tone with red logo			
On card	$5-6	$10-13	$20-25
Loose	$4-5	$8-10	$15-20

A 1990's-era brass logo band bracelet.

Item	VG	EX	NM
Earrings			
Icon with sterling-silver posts			
Ace Frehley	$3-4	$6-8	$12-15
Peter Criss	$3-4	$6-8	$12-15
Paul Stanley	$3-4	$6-8	$12-15
Gene Simmons	$3-4	$6-8	$12-15
Necklaces			
Each member			
Icon, sterling silver, 20"	$10-11	$20-23	$40-45
Icon, pendant style	$6-8	$13-15	$25-30
Signature, on card	$19-25	$38-50	$75-100
Signature, loose	$13-19	$25-38	$50-75
Logo styles			
14k gold	$8-9	$15-18	$30-35
Gold tone, black, blue, green or red logo			
Carded	$8-9	$15-18	$30-35
Loose	$5-6	$10-13	$20-25
Silver tone, black, blue, green or red logo			
Carded	$8-9	$15-18	$30-35
Loose	$5-6	$10-13	$20-25

Item	VG	EX	NM
Rings			
Icons, sterling silver cigar band	$5-6	$10-13	$20-25
Logo all around, sterling silver	$10-11	$20-23	$40-45
Logo, black, on card	$11-13	$23-25	$45-50
Logo, black	$6-8	$13-15	$25-30
Logo, sterling silver, large link	$8-9	$15-18	$30-35
Logo, sterling silver, small link	$5-6	$10-13	$20-25
Logo, sterling silver, split shank	$5-6	$10-13	$20-25
Logo in oval	$3-3	$5-7	$10-13
Stick pin, face style			
Each member	$14-15	$28-30	$55-60
Gold tone logo style, black, blue, green or red logo			
Love Gun card	$8-9	$15-18	$30-35
Loose	$4-5	$8-10	$15-20
Silver tone logo style, black, blue, green or red logo			
Love Gun card	$8-9	$15-18	$30-35
Loose	$4-5	$8-10	$15-20

Jump suit, crewmember

Item	VG	EX	NM
Farewell tour	$50-63	$100-125	$200-250

Key chain

Item	VG	EX	NM
Each original member			
Australian (no Peter Criss)	$16-19	$33-38	$65-75
Coin	$1-2	$3-4	$5-8
Japanese promo, 1996	$10-13	$20-25	$40-50
Love Gun face	$16-19	$33-38	$65-75

Psycho Circus Tour metal key chain.

Item	VG	EX	NM
Psycho Circus	$1-2	$3-4	$5-8
Solo LP	$31-38	$63-75	$125-150
Group styles			
Kinetic Art			
Solo faces	4-5	8-10	15-20
Leather			
Logo	$3-4	$7-8	$13-16
Logo on key tab (fits on belt)	$3-4	$7-8	$13-16
Logo with guitars	$2-3	$5-6	$9-12
Oblong logo, with icons	$2-3	$5-6	$9-12
Square logo with icons	$2-3	$5-6	$9-12
Square logo with large icons	$2-3	$5-6	$9-12
Metal			
Round with KISS and Psycho Circus logos	$2-3	$4-5	$7-10

Item	VG	EX	NM
Logo and icons charms	$3-4	$7-8	$13-16
Psycho Circus tour, pewter	$2-3	$4-5	$8-10
Rubber			
Icons on star	$1-2	$2-3	$3-6
Solo faces	$1-1	$2-3	$3-5

KISS ARMY kits

Item	VG	EX	NM
Pre-Destroyer	$31-38	$63-75	$125-150
Destroyer	$13-19	$25-38	$50-75
Rock and Roll Over	$13-19	$25-38	$50-75
Love Gun	$13-19	$25-38	$50-75
Alive II/Double Platinum	$13-19	$25-38	$50-75
Solos	$13-19	$25-38	$50-75
The Elder (Australian)	$31-38	$63-75	$125-150

KISS Army News

Item	VG	EX	NM
Vol. 1, #1, #2, #3	$2-3	$5-6	$9-12
Vol.2, #1, #2, #3; Vol. 3, #1, #2	$3-4	$6-8	$12-15
Vol. 4, #1, #2	$4-5	$8-10	$15-20
1980, Eric Carr cover	$4-5	$8-10	$15-20
1980, Unmasked cover	$4-5	$8-10	$15-20
1981, Australia cover	$4-5	$8-10	$15-20
Army enlistment card	$1-2	$2-3	$3-6
Envelope, empty	$1-2	$2-3	$3-6

Lava lamp

Item	VG	EX	NM
Boxed	$19-25	$38-50	$75-100

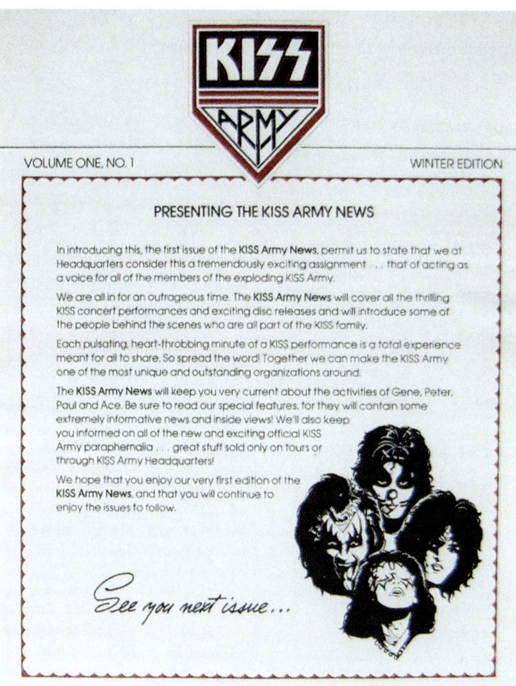

KISS ARMY

VOLUME ONE, NO. 1

WINTER EDITION

PRESENTING THE KISS ARMY NEWS

In introducing this, the first issue of the **KISS Army News**, permit us to state that we at Headquarters consider this a tremendously exciting assignment . . . that of acting as a voice for all of the members of the exploding KISS Army.

We are all in for an outrageous time. The **KISS Army News** will cover all the thrilling KISS concert performances and exciting disc releases and will introduce some of the people behind the scenes who are all part of the KISS family.

Each pulsating, heart-throbbing minute of a KISS performance is a total experience meant for all to share. So spread the word! Together we can make the KISS Army one of the most unique and outstanding organizations around.

The **KISS Army News** will keep you very current about the activities of Gene, Peter, Paul and Ace. Be sure to read our special features, for they will contain some extremely informative news and inside views! We'll also keep you informed on all of the new and exciting official KISS Army paraphernalia . . . great stuff sold only on tours or through KISS Army Headquarters!

We hope that you enjoy our very first edition of the **KISS Army News**, and that you will continue to enjoy the issues to follow.

See you next issue...

KISS Army News Volume One, Number One.

Item	VG	EX	NM
License plate			
World Domination	$2-3	$4-5	$7-10
License plate frame			
Honk if you're a KISS fan, plastic, red on white, or white on black	$1-2	$3-4	$5-8
Light string	$3-4	$5-8	$10-15
Lighter, disposable			
Alive II	$1-1	$2-2	$3-4
Destroyer Pose	$1-1	$2-2	$3-4
Logo	$1-1	$2-2	$3-4
Rock and Roll Over	$1-1	$2-2	$3-4
Solo Faces	$1-1	$2-2	$3-4
Lighter, refillable			
Each member			
Psycho Circus, Zippo			
Boxed	$6-8	$13-15	$25-30
Loose	$4-5	$8-10	$15-20
Solo art, Zippo			
Boxed	$6-8	$13-15	$25-30
Loose	$4-5	$8-10	$15-20
Group			
Silver with black logo, Zippo			
Boxed	$5-6	$10-13	$20-25
Loose	$3-4	$5-8	$10-15

Lava lamp.

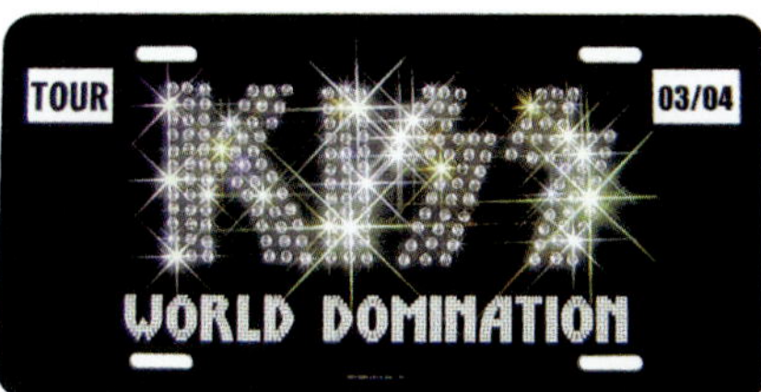

World Domination Tour license plate.

Ten-light string.

Item	VG	EX	NM
Alive II	$2-3	$4-5	$7-10
Destroyer (bootleg)	$2-3	$4-5	$7-10
Silver with KISS Army Shield, Zippo			
Boxed	$5-6	$10-13	$20-25
Loose	$3-4	$5-8	$10-15
KISS Army, vintage style	$1-2	$3-4	$5-8
KISS My Ass, vintage style	$1-2	$3-4	$5-8
KISS Icons Psycho Circus, Zippo			
Boxed	$6-8	$13-15	$25-30
Loose	$4-5	$8-10	$15-20
Psycho Circus Wagon, Zippo			
Boxed	$6-8	$13-15	$25-30
Loose	$4-5	$8-10	$15-20
Psycho Circus, boxed set of six, Limited to 200, Zippo	$45-50	$90-100	$180-200
Psycho Circus, vintage style	$1-2	$3-4	$5-8
Solo box set of four, Zippo	$30-33	$60-65	$120-130
Solo art (not Zippo)	$2-3	$4-5	$7-10

Lunch box/drink containers

Item	VG	EX	NM
Lunch box, 1977	$100-113	$200-225	$400-450
Thermos, 1977	$10-13	$20-25	$40-50
Ace Frehley, 1998 (bootleg)	$3-4	$6-8	$12-15
Peter Criss, 1998 (bootleg)	$3-4	$6-8	$12-15
Paul Stanley, 1998 (bootleg)	$3-4	$6-8	$12-15
Gene Simmons, 1998 (bootleg)	$3-4	$6-8	$12-15
1st LP pose, 1998 (bootleg)	$3-4	$6-8	$12-15

A 1977 lunch box with thermos.

Some Reunion-era lunch boxes, from top left: The Farewell Tour, first LP pose, Destroyer, solo faces, and Love Gun.

A five-piece drink containers set.

Item	VG	EX	NM
Reunion pose, 1998 (bootleg)	$3-4	$6-8	$12-15
ALIVE! 2001			
(with drink container)	$5-6	$10-13	$20-25
Destroyer, 2000			
Box	$4-5	$8-10	$15-20
Drink container (sold separately)	$2-3	$4-5	$8-10
Farewell Tour, 2001			
Box	$4-5	$8-10	$15-20
Drink container (sold separately)	$2-3	$4-5	$8-10
Love Gun, 2001			
Box	$4-5	$8-10	$15-20
Drink container (sold separately)	$2-3	$4-5	$8-10
New York Skyline, 2001			
(with drink container)	$5-6	$10-13	$20-25
The Originals, 2000			
Box	$4-5	$8-10	$15-20
Drink container (sold separately)	$2-3	$4-5	$8-10

Item	VG	EX	NM
Solo faces, 2001			
Box	$4-5	$8-10	$15-20
Drink container (sold separately)	$2-3	$4-5	$8-10
Drink container, boxed set of 5	$11-13	$23-25	$45-50

Makeup kit

Item	VG	EX	NM
KISS Your Face			
Removable with cold cream	$56-63	$113-125	$225-250
Removable with water	$48-54	$95-108	$190-215
Booklet from makeup kit	$6-8	$13-15	$25-30
Boxed, 1998, wig/stencils	$4-5	$8-10	$15-20
Carded, 1997	$1-2	$3-4	$5-8
Carded, Wal-Mart exclusive, small size card	$2-3	$4-5	$7-10

Makeup kit variations, 1997.

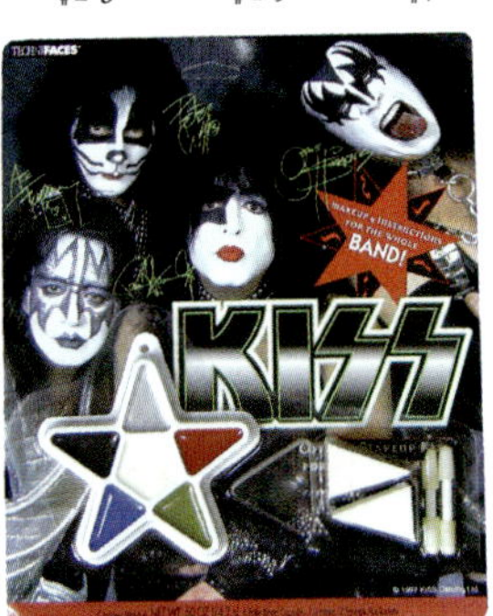

A 1998 boxed makeup kit with wig and stencils.

Makeup kits, 1970s. Rich Vanderwerken collection.

Item	VG	EX	NM
Magazines			
(Magazine covers can be seen at www.kisshall.com)			
All KISS magazines, 1970s			
Award Winning KISS			
Exclusive #1, 1978	$5-6	$10-13	$20-25
Bananas, The Great Kiss-Off	$3-4	$6-8	$12-15
Creem KISS Special	$6-8	$13-15	$25-30
Grooves, #1 and #3	$6-8	$13-15	$25-30
Grooves, #7, #15 and #18	$4-5	$8-10	$15-20
KISS Collector Series,			
Ace, Peter, Paul or Gene cover	$4-5	$8-10	$15-20
KISS Meets the Phantom	$6-8	$13-15	$25-30
KISS Special, "KISS Dead"	$4-5	$8-10	$15-20
Music Life, 1977, Japan			
[cover, pinup, article]	$10-11	$20-23	$40-45
Music Life, 1978, Japan			
[cover, pinup, article]	$10-11	$20-23	$40-45
Official KISS Poster Book	$5-6	$10-13	$20-25
Punk Rock Special	$4-5	$8-10	$15-20
Rock N Roll Special KISS Coll.	$4-5	$8-10	$15-20
Rock On Special "KISS Curse"	$4-5	$8-10	$15-20
Super Rock Awards	$4-5	$8-10	$15-20
Super Teen Special #1	$4-5	$8-10	$15-20
Teen Favorites Presents KISS	$4-5	$8-10	$15-20
Teen Machine Presents KISS	$4-5	$8-10	$15-20
Teenstar Poster, Paul cover	$4-5	$8-10	$15-20
Teenstar Poster, group cover	$4-5	$8-10	$15-20

Grooves Number One magazine.

KISS Meets the Phantom magazine.

Teen Machine magazine.

Teen Star magazine.

The Best of KISS magazine.

Item	VG	EX	NM
Teen Talk Presents KISS	$4-5	$8-10	$15-20
Teen Throbs, Kiss Kollection	$2-3	$5-6	$9-12
The Best of KISS	$4-5	$8-10	$15-20
TV Superstar KISS Pinup	$2-3	$5-6	$9-12
TV Superstar KISS Mania	$4-5	$8-10	$15-20
TV Superstar KISS Krazy	$4-5	$8-10	$15-20
All KISS magazines, 1980s-90s			
Anabas #4, 1987	$3-4	$6-8	$12-15
Creem Collectors Series KISS	$3-4	$6-8	$12-15
Faces, 1996	$3-4	$6-8	$12-15
KISS Alive, Arena edition	$2-3	$5-6	$9-12
KISS Alive 1990	$2-3	$5-6	$9-12
KISS The Videos	$2-3	$5-6	$9-12
KISS Exposed	$2-3	$5-6	$9-12
KISS Guitarists	$2-3	$5-6	$9-12
KISS Live, 1996 (UK)	$3-4	$6-8	$12-15
KISS Nation	$5-6	$10-13	$20-25
KISS on the Record	$2-3	$5-6	$9-12
KISS Rocks the World, Arena edition	$2-3	$5-6	$9-12
KISS Still on Fire	$2-3	$5-6	$9-12
KISS Tours 1974-1988, The	$3-4	$6-8	$12-15
KISS the Complete History	$2-3	$5-6	$9-12
Le Mag, 1997 (France)	$4-5	$8-10	$15-20
Metal Madness #3, 1989	$2-3	$5-6	$9-12
Metal Madness, The Might and Magic of KISS	$2-3	$5-6	$9-12
Metal Muscle A Tribute To KISS	$2-3	$5-6	$9-12

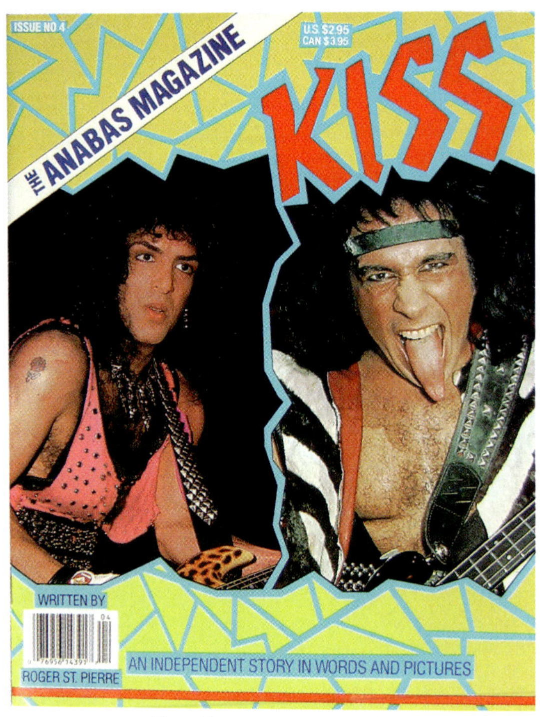

The Anabas Magazine, Issue No. 4.

Creem Collectors series KISS magazine.

Faces Rocks magazine.

KISS Exposed video official magazine.

KISS Live 1974 to 1993 magazine.

Metal Madness, The Might and Magic of KISS magazine.

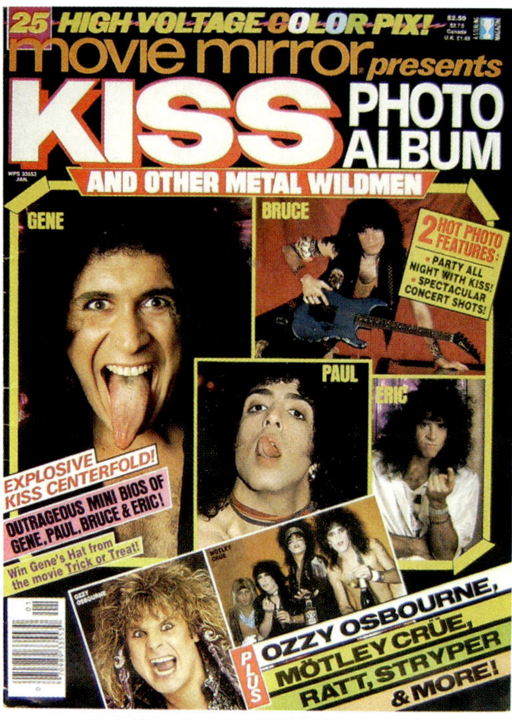

Movie Mirror Presents KISS Photo Album magazine.

Item	VG	EX	NM
Movie Mirror A Tribute To KISS, 1974-1993	$3-4	$6-8	$12-15
Movie Mirror KISS Photo Album	$3-4	$6-8	$12-15
Official KISS Detroit Rock City	$3-4	$6-8	$12-15
Official KISS Psycho Circus Tour	$3-4	$6-8	$12-15
Personality Parade, 1990 #259	$3-4	$6-8	$12-15
RIP Photo Special KISS	$3-4	$6-8	$12-15
Rock Scene, The KISS Collection	$3-4	$6-8	$12-15
Starlog Official KISS Magazine #2	$2-3	$5-6	$9-12
Starline Presents KISS	$2-3	$5-6	$9-12
Superstar	$2-3	$5-6	$9-12
Teen Machine KISS Strikes Back	$2-3	$5-6	$9-12
1989, Teen Throbs, Kiss Kollection	$2-3	$5-6	$9-12
The Brand New KISS	$2-3	$5-6	$9-12
The KISS Kollection	$2-3	$5-6	$9-12
The Might and Magic of KISS	$2-3	$5-6	$9-12
The Videos	$2-3	$5-6	$9-12
TV Superstar KISS Fever	$2-3	$5-6	$9-12
Superstar Facts and Pix	$2-3	$5-6	$9-12
KISS on cover, or articles			
Aquarian Weekly #104 (1975)	$5-6	$10-13	$20-25
Bananas, 1978, #18 [cover, article]	$1-2	$3-4	$5-8
Bass Frontiers 1996, Gene cover	$2-3	$4-5	$7-10
1979, Bravo, KISS on cover	$3-4	$6-8	$12-15

The Official KISS Detroit Rock City Movie magazine.

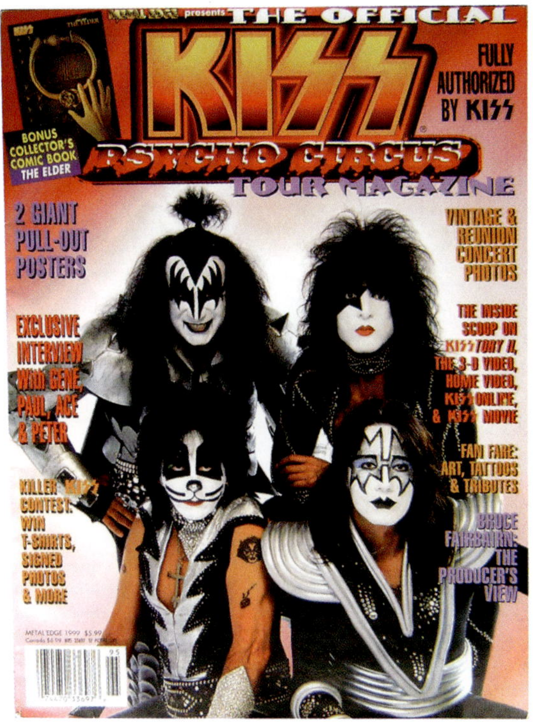

The Official KISS Psycho Circus Tour Magazine.

Starlog Movie Series Presents The Official KISS Magazine, #2.

Starline Presents KISS A Tribute to KISS magazine.

Superstar Facts and Pix KISS and the Other Wild Men of Metal magazine.

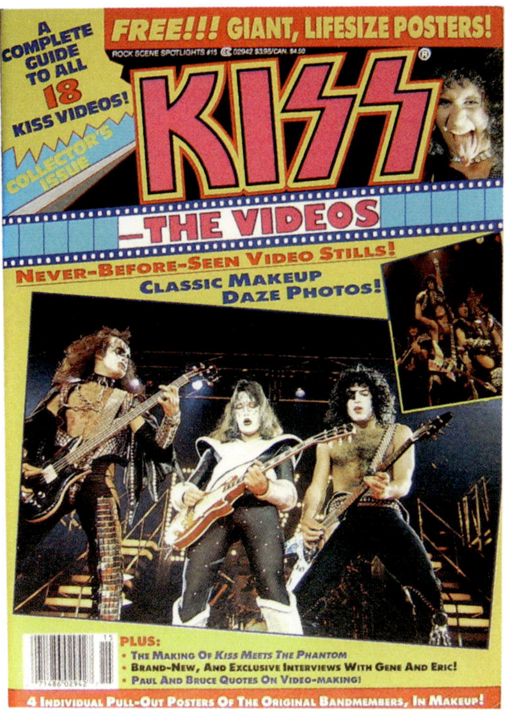

KISS the Videos magazine.

New Wave Rock magazine.

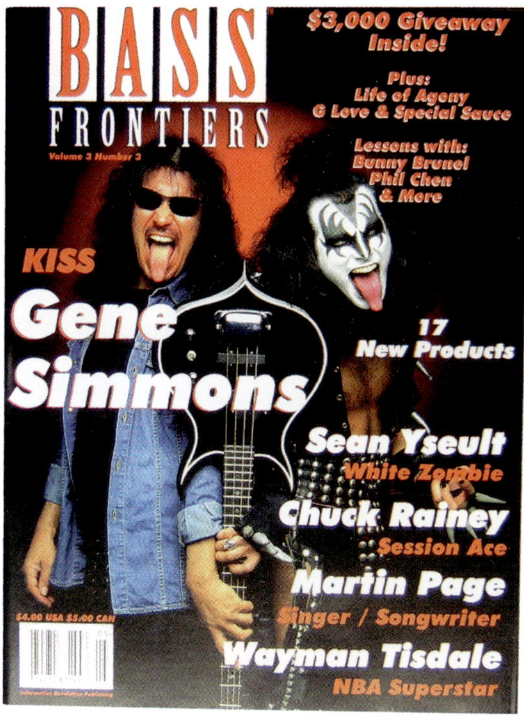

Bass Frontiers magazine.

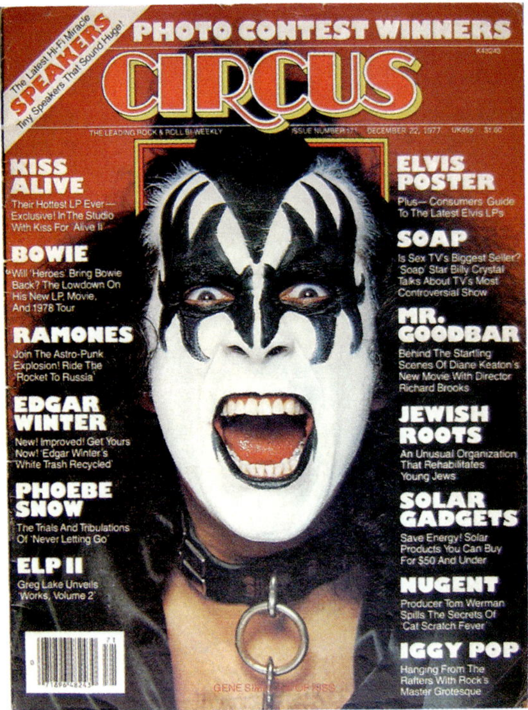

Circus magazine, Dec. 22,1977.

Item	VG	EX	NM
Circus Magazine			
1975, January, #102 [article]	$5-6	$10-13	$20-25
1975, March, #106 [article]	$3-4	$6-8	$12-15
1975, July, #114 [article]	$3-4	$6-8	$12-15
1975, October, #120 [pinup, article]	$3-4	$6-8	$12-15
1975, December, #124 [article, ad]	$3-4	$6-8	$12-15
1975, December, #125 [ad]	$2-3	$4-5	$7-10
1976-1977 KISS specials	$3-4	$6-8	$12-15
1976-1983	$1-2	$3-4	$5-8
1984-1990	$1-2	$2-3	$3-6
1991 to present	$1-1	$1-2	$2-4
Circus' Solid Gold Circus, 1978	$3-4	$6-8	$12-15
Circus Raves	$3-4	$6-8	$12-15
Creem magazine			
1974, May [article]	$4-5	$8-10	$15-20
1974, June [article]	$4-5	$8-10	$15-20
1974, October [article]	$4-5	$8-10	$15-20
1975, April [article]	$3-4	$6-8	$12-15
1975, July [article]	$3-4	$6-8	$12-15
1975, August [article]	$3-4	$6-8	$12-15
1975, December [article]	$3-4	$6-8	$12-15
1976-1977 KISS specials	$4-5	$8-10	$15-20
1976-1981	$1-2	$3-4	$5-8
Discoveries	$2-3	$4-5	$7-10
Entertainment Weekly	$1-2	$3-4	$5-8
Faces Rock	$1-2	$3-4	$5-8

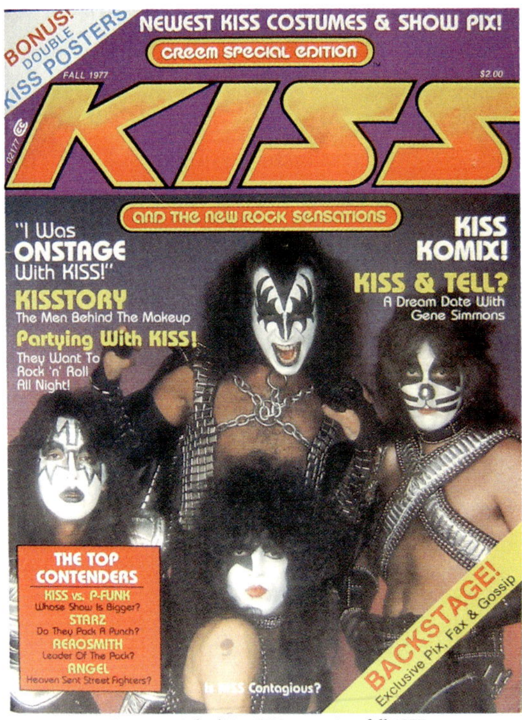

Creem special-edition KISS magazine, fall 1977.

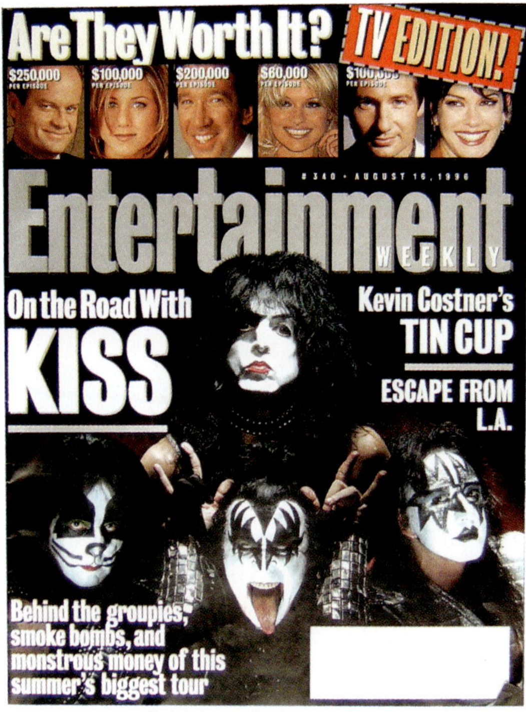

Entertainment Weekly magazine.

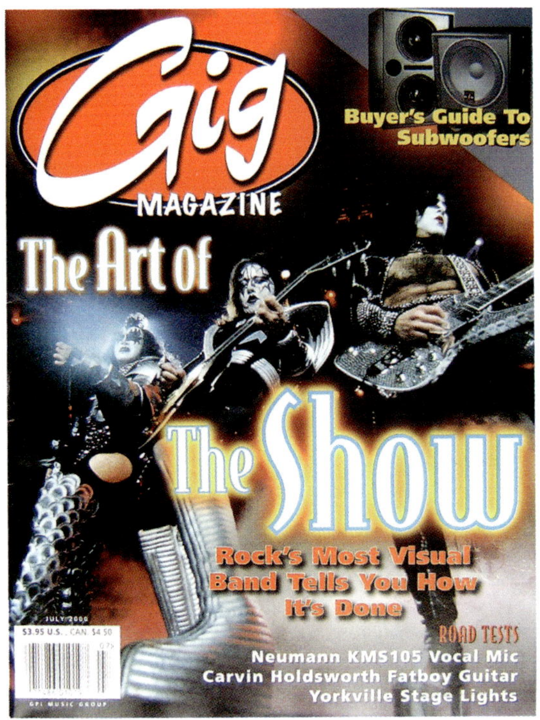

Gig Magazine.

Go Figure! Number One magazine.

Go Figure! magazine.

Guitar World magazine, October 1999.

Item	VG	EX	NM
Forbes	$1-2	$3-4	$5-8
Gig	$1-2	$2-3	$3-6
Goldmine	$2-3	$4-5	$7-10
Go Figure!	$1-2	$3-4	$5-8
Guitar	$1-2	$3-4	$5-8
Guitar Player	$1-2	$3-4	$5-8
Guitar School	$1-2	$3-4	$5-8
Guitar World	$1-2	$3-4	$5-8
Hard Rock	$1-2	$3-4	$5-8
High Voltage	$1-2	$2-3	$3-6
Hit Parader			
1975, October [article]	$3-4	$6-8	$12-15
1976-1983 with articles only	$1-2	$3-4	$5-8
1977-1979 on cover	$2-3	$5-6	$9-12
1977, March [cover, article]	$2-3	$5-6	$9-12
1984-1990	$1-2	$2-3	$3-6
Hit Parader, 1991 to 1995	$1-1	$1-2	$2-4
Hit Parader, 1996-present	$1-2	$3-4	$5-8
Hit Parader Heavy Metal Awards	$1-2	$2-3	$3-6
Hit Parader Heavy Metal Heroes	$1-2	$2-3	$3-6
Hit Parader Heavy Metal Hot Shots	$1-2	$2-3	$3-6
Hit Parader Heavy Metal Stars	$1-2	$2-3	$3-6
Hit Parader's Legends of Heavy Metal	$1-2	$3-4	$5-8
Hit Parader's Top 100 Metal Albums	$1-2	$2-3	$3-6
Hit Parader's Top 100 Metal Stars	$1-2	$2-3	$3-6

Heavy Metal Heroes magazine, Bon Jovi vs. KISS.

Hit Parader Heavy Metal Heroes, KISS vs. Motley Crue.

Incite magazine, February 2000.

Marshall Law magazine, winter 1997.

The Official KISS Alive Worldwide 1996/1997 Tour Magazine.

The Official KISS Rocks The World Reunion Tour magazine.

Metal Muscle magazine, A Tribute To KISS.

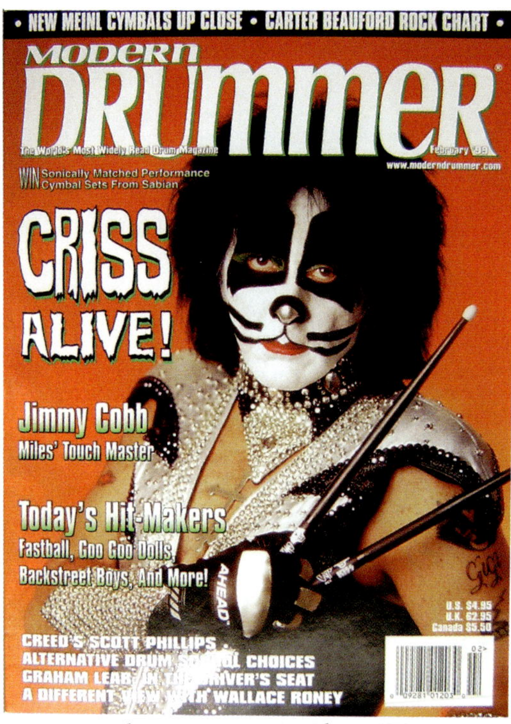

Modern Drummer magazine, February 1999.

Item	VG	EX	NM
Hit Parader Yearbook	$1-2	$3-4	$5-8
Incite	$1-2	$2-3	$3-6
Kerrang	$1-2	$2-3	$3-6
Lighting Dimensions	$1-2	$3-4	$5-8
Live Wire	$1-2	$3-4	$5-8
Marshall Law	$1-2	$2-3	$3-6
Metal, The Best of	$1-2	$2-3	$3-6
Metal Edge, up to March 1996	$1-2	$2-3	$3-6
Metal Edge, April 1996 to present	$1-2	$3-4	$5-8
Metal Madness			
1989, #3 [KISS Special]	$3-4	$6-8	$12-15
All others	$1-2	$2-3	$3-6
Metal Muscle	$1-2	$3-4	$5-8
Metal Muscle: Megastars of Metal Special	$1-2	$2-3	$3-6
Modern Drummer	$1-2	$3-4	$5-8
Movie World	$1-2	$3-4	$5-8
Music Life (Japan)			
1970s	$10-11	$20-23	$40-45
1990s	$8-9	$15-18	$30-35
Musical Express (newspaper)			
1974, March [cover]	$11-13	$23-25	$45-50
Musician	$1-2	$3-4	$5-8
Mu Zikus (Germany)	$4-5	$8-10	$15-20
New Wave Super Groups, the Rise of Kiss	$3-4	$6-8	$12-15
OKEJ	$4-5	$8-10	$15-20

Prowl, The Official Magazine of the Plymouth Prowler Club.

Rock Special KISSue magazine, November 1976.

The KISS Tours 1974-1988 magazine.

Item	VG	EX	NM
People			
1979, March [cover]	$4-5	$8-10	$15-20
1991, January [article]	$2-3	$5-6	$9-12
Playboy	$1-2	$3-4	$5-8
POV	$1-2	$3-4	$5-8
Proview	$1-2	$3-4	$5-8
Prowl	$1-2	$3-4	$5-8
Ram	$2-3	$5-6	$9-12
Record Review	$1-2	$3-4	$5-8
Record World	$2-3	$5-6	$9-12
RIP	$1-2	$2-3	$3-6
Rock			
1976, November, [cover, article]	$2-3	$5-6	$9-12
1977-78	$1-2	$3-4	$5-8
1979	$2-3	$5-6	$9-12
1988	$1-2	$3-4	$5-8
Rock Awards			
1978, #1, [cover, pinup, article]	$4-5	$8-10	$15-20
1979, Summer [cover, article]	$2-3	$5-6	$9-12
Rock Beat	$1-2	$2-3	$3-6
Rock Fever	$1-2	$2-3	$3-6
Rock Fever Awards	$2-3	$5-6	$9-12
Rock Gossip	$2-3	$5-6	$9-12
Rock Hard	$3-4	$6-8	$12-15
Rock Mania	$2-3	$5-6	$9-12

Item	VG	EX	NM
Rock N Roll Special			
1978, Winter #1 [article]	$1-2	$3-4	$5-8
1979, Spring #2, [cover, article]	$2-3	$5-6	$9-12
Rock On Special	$2-3	$5-6	$9-12
Rock Poster Magazine	$1-2	$2-3	$3-6
Rock Report	$1-2	$3-4	$5-8
Rock Scene			
1975-1981 covers	$2-3	$5-6	$9-12
1975-1990	$1-2	$3-4	$5-8
Rock Scene, the Best of			
1978, #1 [cover, article]	$2-3	$5-6	$9-12
1988, #4 [cover, article]	$1-2	$3-4	$5-8
1989 #6 [article]	$1-2	$2-3	$3-6
Rock Scene's Metal Mania	$1-2	$3-4	$5-8
Rock Scene's Metal Mania, the Best of			
1987, #2 [cover, article]	$1-2	$3-4	$5-8
Rock Scene Presents			
Concert Shots	$1-2	$2-3	$3-6
Rock Scene Concert Shots, the Best			
of 1987, #1 [article]	$1-2	$2-3	$3-6
Rock Scene Spotlights	$3-4	$6-8	$12-15
Rock Spectacular	$2-3	$5-6	$9-12
Rock World			
1979, Summer [cover, article]	$2-3	$5-6	$9-12
1985, January [article]	$1-2	$2-3	$3-6

Item	VG	EX	NM
Rock 79	$2-3	$5-6	$9-12
Rocket			
1978, March #1, [cover, article]	$2-3	$5-6	$9-12
Others	$1-2	$3-4	$5-8
Rolling Stone	$1-2	$2-3	$3-6
Screamer	$1-2	$2-3	$3-6
Shout	$1-2	$2-3	$3-6
Sixteen, 1970s	$2-3	$4-5	$7-10
Smash Hits Presents Metalix	$2-3	$4-5	$7-10
Song Hits			
1977, December [cover]	$3-4	$6-8	$12-15
1978, Fall [cover, article]	$3-4	$6-8	$12-15
1979, February [cover]	$4-5	$8-10	$15-20
1982, April [cover]	$4-5	$8-10	$15-20
1983, June [cover]	$4-5	$8-10	$15-20
Sounds	$2-3	$5-6	$9-12
Spectacular	$1-2	$3-4	$5-8
Spin	$2-3	$4-5	$7-10
Star Line Tribute To Kiss	$3-4	$6-8	$12-15
Star	$1-2	$3-4	$5-8
Super Rock	$1-2	$3-4	$5-8
Super Rock Awards	$3-4	$6-8	$12-15
Super Rock Spectacular	$2-3	$5-6	$9-12
Super Teen Photo Album	$1-2	$2-3	$3-6
Teen Bag	$1-2	$3-4	$5-8
Teen Beat	$2-3	$4-5	$7-10
Teen Machine	$2-3	$5-6	$9-12

Item	VG	EX	NM
Teen Stars Photo Album	$1-2	$3-4	$5-8
Teen Throbs	$2-3	$5-6	$9-12
Time Off	$1-2	$3-4	$5-8
Tongue	$1-2	$2-3	$3-6
TV Guide			
1978, Phantoms ad	$1-2	$3-4	$5-8
1998, Halloween issue	$0-1	$1-2	$1-3
TV Week (Australian), 1980, 11/8 [cover]	$9-10	$18-20	$35-40
Zoo World	$5-6	$10-13	$20-25

Magnets

1/2" thick x 4" square (approximate)			
Logo with band faces inside	$2-3	$4-5	$7-10
Psycho Circus clown	$1-1	$2-3	$3-5
Psycho Circus Wagon	$1-1	$2-3	$3-5
Psycho Circus faces	$1-1	$2-3	$3-5
Reunion standing pose	$2-3	$4-5	$7-10
Reunion pose with logo	$2-3	$4-5	$7-10
3-inch x 4-inch			
Hottest Band…	$1-1	$1-3	$2-5
You Wanted The Best…	$1-1	$1-3	$2-5
Red logo	$1-1	$1-3	$2-5
KISS My Ass artwork	$1-1	$1-3	$2-5
Solo faces around logo	$1-1	$1-3	$2-5
Reunion pose squatting	$1-1	$1-3	$2-5
Reunion shot upper torsos	$1-1	$1-3	$2-5

Magnets: Destroyer sparkle, at top, and Destroyer carriage ride.

Item	VG	EX	NM
Ceramic			
Black logo with first LP photo	$1-1	$1-3	$2-5
Red logo	$1-1	$1-3	$2-5
Other styles			
Alive II	$1-1	$1-3	$2-5
Destroyer Carriage ride	$1-1	$1-3	$2-5
Destroyer Sparkle	$1-1	$1-3	$2-5
Icons	$1-1	$1-3	$2-5
Love Gun	$1-1	$1-3	$2-5
Marauder pose	$1-1	$1-3	$2-5
New York Skyline	$1-1	$1-3	$2-5
Psycho in yellow	$1-1	$1-3	$2-5
Gene face	$1-1	$1-3	$2-5
Set of four solos and one logo	$4-5	$8-10	$15-20
Set of seven mini magnets	$4-5	$8-10	$15-20
Solo faces	$1-1	$1-3	$2-5
Solo faces, individual magnets on one blister pack	$2-3	$5-6	$9-12

Models

Item	VG	EX	NM
Each member			
Destroyer long box	$4-5	$8-10	$15-20
Tan box, Toys R Us exclusive	$3-4	$6-8	$12-15
Built	$1-2	$3-4	$5-8
Chevy van, 1978			
In box, unbuilt	$31-38	$63-75	$125-150
Built, with box	$13-15	$25-30	$50-60
Box only	$9-11	$18-23	$35-45
Model only	$4-5	$8-10	$15-20

A 1978 Chevy van model.

Mouse pad, Reunion photo.

Item	VG	EX	NM
Mouse pads			
Alive II gatefold (bootleg)	$2-3	$4-5	$7-10
Cartoon solo faces (bootleg)	$2-3	$4-5	$7-10
KISS LP pose (bootleg)	$2-3	$4-5	$7-10
Psycho Circus	$2-3	$5-6	$9-12
Psycho in yellow	$2-3	$5-6	$9-12
Reunion photo	$2-3	$5-6	$9-12
Rock and Roll Over (bootleg)	$2-3	$4-5	$7-10
Solo faces	$2-3	$5-6	$9-12
You Wanted The Best (Bootleg)	$2-3	$4-5	$7-10
"N" the Box (Jack in the box)	$4-5	$8-10	$15-20
Notebooks			
Ace Frehley with signature	$10-11	$20-23	$40-45
Peter Criss with signature	$10-11	$20-23	$40-45
Paul Stanley with signature	$10-11	$20-23	$40-45
Gene Simmons with signature	$10-11	$20-23	$40-45
Alive II poster poses	$15-18	$30-35	$60-70
Dynasty poses in flames	$19-25	$38-50	$75-100
Dynasty poses in flames steno pad	$13-15	$25-30	$50-60
Love Gun, "On cubes"	$10-11	$20-23	$40-45
Revenge memo pad	$4-5	$8-10	$15-20
Solo albums collage	$10-11	$20-23	$40-45

"N" the Box, a new version of a jack in the box.

Solo faces notebook paper.

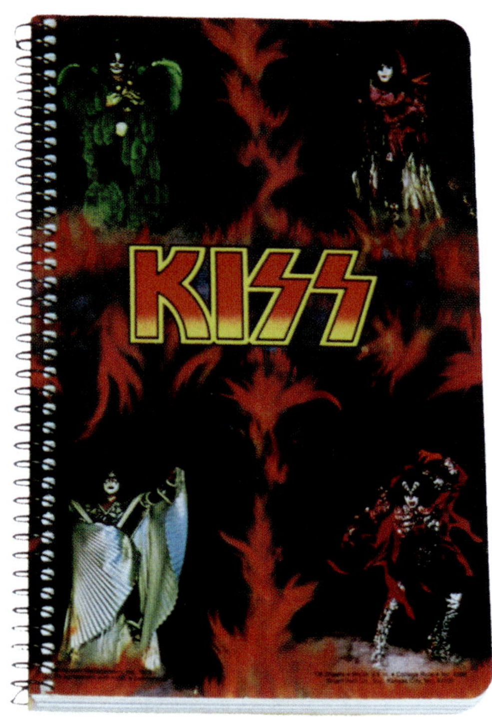

Steno pad, Dynasty poses in flames.

Item	VG	EX	NM
Pajamas			
Children's, 1978	$31-38	$63-75	$125-150
Adults, 1998	$8-10	$15-20	$30-40
Rock And Roll Over, women's bottoms	$2-3	$4-5	$7-10

Men's adult pajamas.

Item	VG	EX	NM
Pencils			
Set of four, sealed	$25-31	$50-63	$100-125
Each member, loose	$3-4	$6-8	$12-15

Some 1970s pencils of each member.

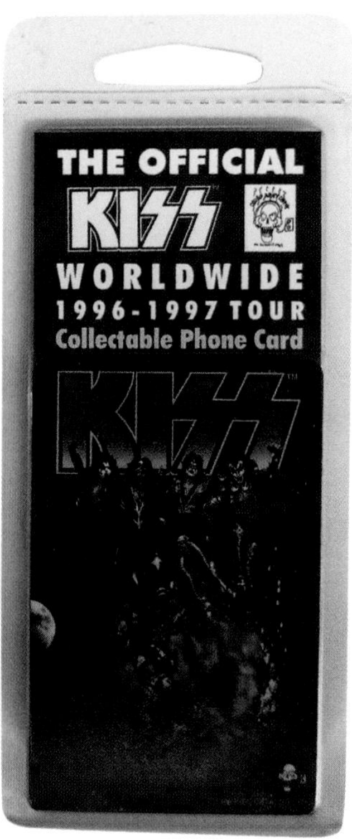

A 1996-97 Reunion tour phone card, KC#1.

Item	VG	EX	NM
PEZ dispensers (bootleg)			
Each member			
Sealed on header card	$5-6	$10-13	$20-25
Loose	$3-4	$6-8	$12-15
Phone cards			
Greatest KISS (promo)	$3-3	$5-6	$10-12
You Wanted The Best,			
(Best Buy promo)	$6-8	$13-15	$25-30
Spencer Gifts exclusives,			
Solo faces (2000)	$4-5	$8-10	$15-20
Convention lithograph (2000)	$4-5	$8-10	$15-20
96-97 Reunion Tour card, KC #1	$4-5	$8-9	$15-18
Gene face, KC #2	$1-2	$2-3	$3-6
Ace face, KC #3	$1-2	$2-3	$3-6
Paul face, KC #4	$1-2	$2-3	$3-6
Peter face, KC #5	$1-2	$2-3	$3-6
Group on bars, KC #6	$1-2	$2-3	$3-6
Peter in chair, KC #7	$1-2	$2-3	$3-6
Gene with wings, KC #8	$1-2	$2-3	$3-6
Paul in flames, KC #9	$1-2	$2-3	$3-6
Ace in pyramids, KC #10	$1-2	$2-3	$3-6

Item	VG	EX	NM
Photographs, official sets			
Auction photo sets			
Set of four	$4-5	$8-10	$15-20
Set of four, Gene and Paul signed	$18-19	$35-38	$70-75
Alive II photos from Alive II LP	$50-55	$100-110	$200-220
Alive II photos from Unmasked LP order sheet (10)	$13-15	$25-30	$50-60
Double Platinum LP set (5)	$6-8	$13-15	$25-30
Rock and Roll Over LP set (5)	$6-8	$13-15	$25-30
Photo fold out set (8 photos)	$9-10	$18-20	$35-40
Promo 8 x 10, 1973-75			
Black and white	$5-6	$10-13	$20-25
Color	$6-8	$13-15	$25-30
Promo 8 x 10, 1976-83			
Black and white	$3-4	$6-8	$12-15
Color	$4-5	$8-10	$15-20
Promo 8 x 10, 1984-95			
Black and white	$1-2	$2-3	$3-6
Color	$2-3	$4-5	$7-10
Promo 8 x 10, 1996-present			
Black and white	$1-2	$2-3	$3-6
Color	$2-3	$4-5	$7-10

Photo fold-out set.

Photo fold-out set, opened.

Item	VG	EX	NM
Pillows			
Dynasty cover art, white on black	$5-6	$10-13	$20-25
Faces with logo, embroidered	$6-8	$13-15	$25-30
KISS logo, on black	$5-6	$10-13	$20-25
Psycho Circus logo, on black	$5-6	$10-13	$20-25
Saw blade logo with signatures	$5-6	$10-13	$20-25
Pillowcases			
Pillow cases, loose (1978)	$13-15	$25-30	$50-60
Asylum	$5-6	$10-13	$20-25
Pinball machine			
Pinball machine	$750-875	$1,500-1,750	$3,000-3,500
Brochure	$13-16	$25-33	$50-65
Instruction booklet/schematics	$5-8	$10-15	$20-30

Pillow, KISS logo, on black.

Asylum pillow case. Jeff Barre collection.

Animalize pins.

Item	VG	EX	NM
Pins			
Ace Frehley solo art, 3"	$5-6	$10-13	$20-25
Peter Criss solo art, 3"	$5-6	$10-13	$20-25
Paul Stanley solo art, 3"	$5-6	$10-13	$20-25
Gene Simmons solo art, 3"	$5-6	$10-13	$20-25

Asylum pins.

Item	VG	EX	NM
Alive III (promo from Alive III autograph parties)	$1-1	$1-3	$2-5
Animalize era	$1-2	$2-3	$3-6
Asylum era	$1-2	$2-3	$3-6
Crazy Nights	$1-2	$2-3	$3-6

Lick It Up pins.

Item	VG	EX	NM
I Was There (Alive II recording)	$10-11	$20-23	$40-45
Lick It Up era	$1-2	$2-3	$3-6
Logo, orange Musicland promo	$2-3	$4-5	$7-10
Logo, Flashing	$2-3	$4-5	$7-10

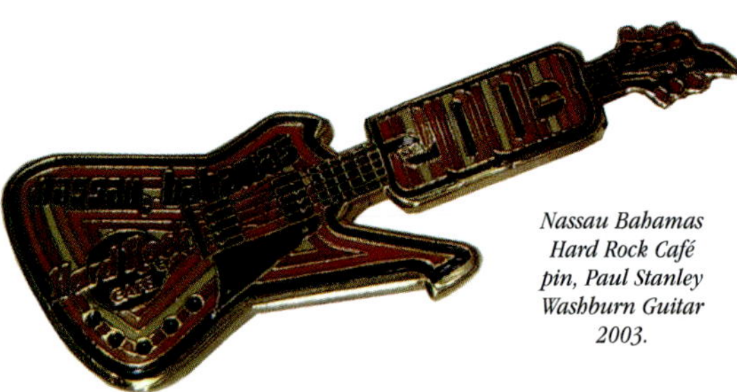

Nassau Bahamas Hard Rock Café pin, Paul Stanley Washburn Guitar 2003.

Item	VG	EX	NM
Psycho Circus and logo	$1-2	$2-3	$3-6
Rock And Roll Over, 3"	$1-2	$3-4	$5-8
Sphinx with logo	$1-2	$2-3	$3-6
WPLJ Radio Salutes Kiss, Dec. 14, 15, 16, 1977	$5-6	$10-13	$20-25
Sterling silver with collectable tin container			
Icons guitar pick	$3-4	$6-8	$12-15
Psycho Circus guitar pick	$3-4	$6-8	$12-15
Hard Rock Café			
1999 promo, Japan	$10-13	$20-25	$40-50
On-line only pins	$10-13	$20-25	$40-50
USA Café Series 1 (12 different)	$4-5	$8-10	$15-20
USA Café Series 2 (20 different)	$4-5	$8-10	$15-20
Japan Series 1 (8 different)	$10-13	$20-25	$40-50
Japan Series 2 (7 different)	$4-5	$8-10	$15-20
Nassau Bahamas Washburn Guitar 2003	$4-5	$8-10	$15-20

Hard Rock Café pin, USA Café Series 1, Las Vegas.

Item	VG	EX	NM
Plates			
KISSmas			
8-1/2"	$6-8	$13-15	$25-30
3-1/4"	$3-4	$6-8	$12-15
Lightning background			
Proof plate, signed	$63-75	$125-150	$250-300
10-1/4" signed (1,000)	$38-50	$75-100	$150-200
8-1/4" (10,000)	$6-8	$13-15	$25-30
3-1/4"	$3-4	$6-8	$12-15
Psycho Circus			
8-1/2" (10,000)	$8-9	$15-18	$30-35
3-1/4"	$4-5	$8-9	$15-18
3-D (5,000)	$3-4	$5-8	$10-15
Pool cues			
Alive/Worldwide	$10-13	$20-25	$40-50
Icons	$6-8	$13-15	$25-30
Poster Art			
Sealed	$125-150	$250-300	$500-600
Loose	$19-25	$38-50	$75-100

A 1977 General Mills fun group Poster Art A.

A 1977 General Mills fun group Poster Art B.

Item	VG	EX	NM
Posters			
With makeup, retail			
Ace Frehley, Peter Criss, Paul Stanley or Gene Simmons			
Motorcycle pose	$4-5	$8-10	$15-20
Alive II, stage pose	$6-8	$13-15	$25-30
Alive II, stage pose (smaller version 1-1/2' x 2')	$3-4	$6-8	$12-15
Solo art	$19-25	$38-50	$75-100
Double Platinum, silver Mylar	$6-8	$13-15	$25-30
Dynasty costume	$4-5	$8-10	$15-20
Mosaic	$2-3	$4-5	$7-10
Group			
1975 band in concert	$9-10	$18-20	$35-40
1976 black light	$15-19	$30-38	$60-75
Alive II, gatefold photo	$4-5	$8-10	$15-20
Army, mural poster	$3-4	$6-8	$12-15
Comic pages	$2-3	$5-6	$9-12
Fog, Peter with knife	$16-19	$33-38	$65-75
Dressed To Kill, airbrush	$2-3	$5-6	$9-12
Destroyer, album cover	$4-5	$8-10	$15-20
Destroyer, foil	$8-9	$15-18	$30-35
Destroyer, silver Mylar	$5-8	$10-15	$20-30
Dynasty album cover, black print	$8-9	$15-18	$30-35
Dynasty w/red lettering, small	$3-4	$6-8	$12-15
Dynasty w/red lettering, large	$3-4	$6-8	$12-15
Eyes Closed, 1976	$15-19	$30-38	$60-75
Jumbo collage, 1976	$15-19	$30-38	$60-75

A 1977 motorcycle poster.

A 1976 black light poster.

A 1979 Dynasty poster with black print.

A 1976 Eyes Closed poster.

Item	VG	EX	NM
Jumbo KISS Army, 1977	$15-19	$30-38	$60-75
Jumbo Love Gun, 1977	$15-19	$30-38	$60-75
Locker Art, (two different versions)			
Comic art	$1-2	$3-4	$5-8
Not Dead Yet	$1-2	$3-4	$5-8
Logo, black light	$2-3	$5-6	$9-12
Love Gun, album cover	$4-5	$8-10	$15-20
Love Gun, foil	$8-9	$15-18	$30-35
Love Gun, silver Mylar	$3-4	$6-8	12-15
Monster with Gene boots	$2-3	$5-6	$9-12
Motorcycles, group	$8-9	$15-18	$30-35

A 1977 jumbo KISS Army poster.

A 1977 jumbo Love Gun poster.

A 1978 black light pinball poster.

Item	VG	EX	NM
New York skyline	$8-9	$15-18	$30-35
Pinball, 1978, black light	$50-63	$100-125	$200-250
Psycho Circus, door poster	$2-3	$5-6	$9-12
Psycho Circus, glows in the dark	$13-19	$25-38	$50-75
Psycho Circus, mural	$3-4	$6-8	$12-15
Solo art, black light	$2-3	$5-6	$9-12
Solo art, pre framed	$6-8	$13-15	$25-30
Solo covers, combined	$4-5	$8-10	$15-20
Solo covers, velvet	$2-3	$5-6	$9-12

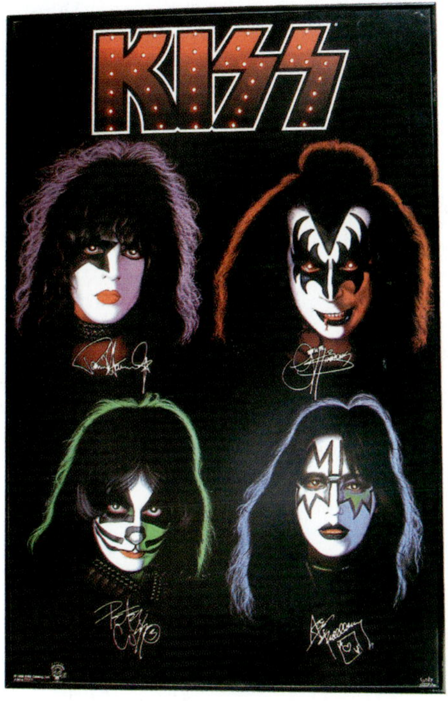

LED-light poster, 1978, solo faces with logo, by Funky.

Item	VG	EX	NM
Superheroes	$6-8	$13-15	$25-30
The Second Coming, 1997	$1-2	$3-4	$5-8
Unmasked, album cover	$4-5	$8-10	$15-20
U.S. Tour 76	$9-10	$18-20	$35-40
U.S. Tour (reissue)	$4-5	$8-10	$15-20
Vancouver, Millennium show	$2-3	$4-5	$7-10
You Wanted The Best, black light	$3-4	$6-8	$12-15
Posters, metal			
Rock And Roll Over	$4-5	$8-10	$15-20
Solo faces	$4-5	$8-10	$15-20
Posters, LED Lighted			
You Wanted The Best…	$31-38	$63-75	$125-150
Solo faces with logo	$31-38	$63-75	$125-150
Posters without makeup, retail			
Any	$4-5	$8-10	$15-20

Poster Put Ons

Item	VG	EX	NM
Live II, Love Gun, US Tour '76			
Sealed	$3-4	$6-8	$12-15
Loose	$1-2	$3-4	$5-7

Promotional items

Item	VG	EX	NM
Promotional, bin divider			
Crazy Nights	$5-6	$10-13	$20-25
Dynasty	$5-6	$10-13	$20-25

A FOX TV Hershey KISS.

Promotional mobile display, Double Platinum logo. Jeff Barre collection.

Promotional mobile display, Double Platinum arrow. Jeff Barre collection.

Item	VG	EX	NM
Promotional, flats (chronological)			
KISS (may not exist)	$10-13	$20-25	$40-50
Hotter Than Hell (may not exist)	$10-13	$20-25	$40-50
Dressed To Kill (may not exist)	$10-13	$20-25	$40-50
Alive!	$10-13	$20-25	$40-50
Destroyer	$6-8	$13-15	$25-30
The Originals	$10-13	$20-25	$40-50
Rock And Roll Over	$6-8	$13-15	$25-30
Love Gun (very common)	$1-2	$3-4	$5-8
Alive II	$6-8	$13-15	$25-30
Double Platinum	$6-8	$13-15	$25-30
Ace Frehley	$5-6	$10-13	$20-25
Peter Criss	$5-6	$10-13	$20-25
Paul Stanley	$5-6	$10-13	$20-25
Gene Simmons	$5-6	$10-13	$20-25
Dynasty	$5-6	$10-13	$20-25
Unmasked	$5-6	$10-13	$20-25
(Music From) The Elder	$6-8	$13-15	$25-30
Creatures of the Night	$6-8	$13-15	$25-30
Lick It Up	$1-2	$3-4	$5-8
Animalize	$1-2	$3-4	$5-8
Asylum	$1-2	$3-4	$5-8
Crazy Nights	$1-2	$3-4	$5-8
Smashes, Thrashes, & Hits	$1-2	$3-4	$5-8
Hot In The Shade	$1-2	$3-4	$5-8
Revenge	$1-2	$2-3	$3-6
Alive III	$1-2	$2-3	$3-6
MTV Unplugged	$1-2	$2-3	$3-6

Party invitation, Las Vegas Palms after party.

Promotional Paul Stanley Washburn guitars, 8 x 10.

Promotional poster, concert venue specific, Oct. 18, 1996.

A promotional Gibson wall display.

Item	VG	EX	NM
You Wanted The Best...	$1-2	$2-3	$3-6
Greatest KISS	$1-2	$2-3	$3-6
Psycho Circus	$1-2	$2-3	$3-6
Psycho Circus, Linticular artwork	$6-8	$13-15	$25-30
Promotional, miscellaneous			
Clipboard, Japan	$25-31	$50-63	$100-125
Hot in the Shade Pyramid			
Boxed	$69-75	$138-150	$275-300
Loose	$19-25	$38-50	$75-100
Halloween KISS from Fox TV (Big Hershey KISS)	$13-19	$25-38	$50-75
Key chain, silver-tone guitar pick	$4-5	$8-10	$15-20
Kiss On Sale end cap display (Destroyer art)	$6-8	$13-15	$25-30
Kiss Platinum Express Card, folder, and envelope	$138-150	$275-300	$550-600
Matches, Creatures Of The Night	$10-13	$20-25	$40-50
Party Invitation, Las Vegas Palms after party	$6-8	$13-15	$25-30
Phantoms movie lobby cards	$13-19	$25-38	$50-75
Ruler, KISS Love Gun	$38-50	$75-100	$150-200
Promotional, mobiles			
Alive II	$94-100	$188-200	$375-400
Alive II arrow shape	$20-25	$40-50	$80-100
Destroyer	$38-44	$75-88	$150-175
Double Platinum, arrow shape	$20-25	$40-50	$80-100
Double Platinum, KISS logo	$20-25	$40-50	$80-100

Promotional poster, Paul Stanley, Washburn guitars.

Promotional poster, Paul Stanley, Washburn Millennium.

Promotional Coins poster.

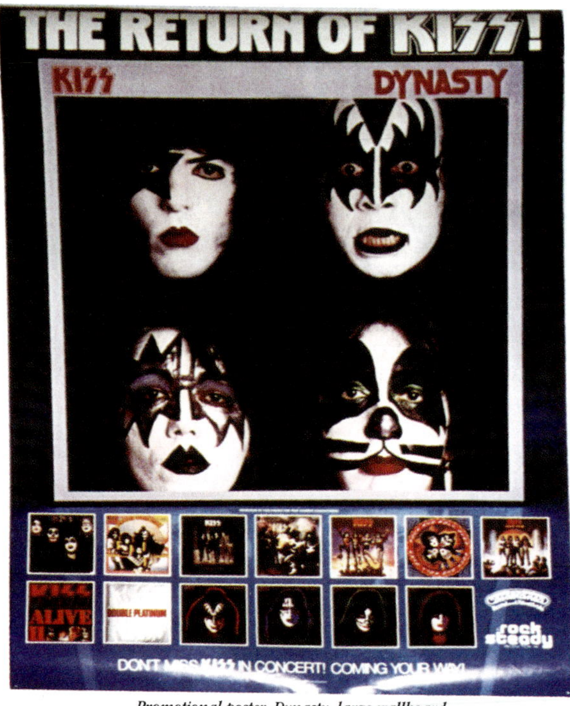

Promotional poster, Dynasty, large wallboard.
Jeff Barre collection.

Promotional poster, (Music from) The Elder.
Jeff Barre Collection.

Item	VG	EX	NM
Hotter Than Hell	$56-63	$113-125	$225-250
Reunion Tour logo	$3-4	$6-8	$12-15
Solo LPs, arrow shape	$20-25	$40-50	$80-100
Unmasked cube	$31-38	$63-75	$125-150
Viewmaster reel	$25-31	$50-63	$100-125
Promotional, posters/concert venue specific			
1974, any	$175-200	$350-400	$700-800
1975, any	$75-88	$150-175	$300-350
1976-1983	$38-50	$75-100	$150-200
1983-1996	$11-15	$23-30	$45-60
1996-present	$11-15	$23-30	$45-60

Item	VG	EX	NM
Promotional, posters			
1st LP (band in smoke)	$100-113	$200-225	$400-450
Ace Frehley, Gibson guitars	$2-3	$5-6	$9-12
Ace Frehley, Gibson contest	$10-13	$20-25	$40-50
Peter Criss, Ahead Drumsticks			
Stock version	$6-8	$13-15	$25-30
Autographed	$16-18	$33-35	$65-70
Farewell Tour	$6-8	$13-15	$25-30
Peter Criss, DW Drums	$6-8	$13-15	$25-30
Peter Criss, Pearl Drums	$100-113	$200-225	$400-450
Gene Simmons, GHS strings, with Spiro small	$6-8	$13-15	$25-30
Gene Simmons, Ampeg amp	$9-11	$18-23	$35-45
Gene Simmons, Sun Amp	$10-13	$20-25	$40-50
Paul Stanley, Ibanez	$38-44	$75-88	$150-175
Paul Stanley, Washburn Millennium	$3-4	$6-8	$12-15
Paul Stanley, Washburn Black Diamond	$3-4	$6-8	$12-15
Alive II, large wallboard	$20-25	$40-50	$80-100
Alive III, square	$2-3	$5-6	$9-12
Alive III, small	$2-3	$5-6	$9-12
Animalize, discography bottom	$6-8	$13-15	$25-30
Animalize video	$6-8	$13-15	$25-30
Asylum, discography back	$6-8	$13-15	$25-30
Asylum, square	$2-3	$5-6	$9-12
Box set, small	$1-2	$3-4	$5-8
Box set, large	$8-10	$15-20	$30-40
Butterfields Auction	$4-5	$8-10	$15-20

Item	VG	EX	NM
Coins	$4-5	$8-10	$15-20
Convention, official 1995	$2-3	$5-6	$9-12
Crazy Nights, discography back	$4-5	$8-10	$15-20
Creatures of the Night, "Loudest"	$13-15	$25-30	$50-60
Dressed To Kill	$38-44	$75-88	$150-175
Double Platinum, wallboard	$20-25	$40-50	$80-100
Dynasty, foamboard banner	$16-19	$33-38	$65-75
Dynasty, small wallboard	$14-16	$28-33	$55-65
Farewell Tour (w/Eric Singer)	$4-5	$8-10	$15-20
Got Milk?	$4-5	$8-10	$15-20
Got Chocolate Milk?	$4-5	$8-10	$15-20
Greatest KISS	$3-4	$6-8	$12-15
Greatest Kiss, German logo	$9-10	$18-20	$35-40
Dynasty, large wallboard	$20-25	$40-50	$80-100
Hot in the Shade, discography	$3-4	$6-8	$12-15
KISS And Makeup	$4-5	$8-10	$15-20
KISS Killers	$19-25	$38-50	$75-100
KISS Meets The Phantom, video	$5-6	$10-13	$20-25
KISS Mobile, Honda motorcycle	$56-63	$113-125	$225-250
KISS Years promo poster	$1-2	$3-4	$5-8
Lick It Up, square	$4-5	$8-10	$15-20
Magic Market cups	$19-25	$38-50	$75-100
McFarlane window poster	$5-8	$10-15	$20-30
(Music from) The Elder, clear	$25-31	$50-63	$100-125
(Music from) The Elder	$16-19	$33-38	$65-75
P.O.V. magazine	$3-4	$6-8	$12-15
Psycho Circus, horizontal	$4-5	$8-10	$15-20

Item	VG	EX	NM
Revenge logo	$3-4	$6-8	$12-15
Smashes, Thrashes and Hits	$3-4	$6-8	$12-15
Solo LPs, foamboard, 2' x 2'	$20-25	$40-50	$80-100
Solo LPs, Japan	$38-44	$75-88	$150-175
Spin magazine cover, Ace	$5-6	$10-13	$20-25
Spin magazine cover, Peter	$5-6	$10-13	$20-25
Spin magazine cover, Paul	$5-6	$10-13	$20-25
Spin magazine cover, Gene	$5-6	$10-13	$20-25
Spirit of '76, horizontal, with first 5 LPs	$31-38	$63-75	$125-150
Superdome, 1996	$4-5	$8-10	$15-20
Unplugged, discography back	$4-5	$8-10	$15-20
You Wanted The Best	$3-4	$6-8	$12-15
You Wanted The Best, Block Buster Music	$9-11	$18-23	$35-45
Promotional, press kits			
KISS	$150-175	$300-350	$600-700
Hotter Than Hell	$63-75	$125-150	$250-300
Dressed To Kill	$63-75	$125-150	$250-300
Alive! (may not exist)	$31-38	$63-75	$125-150
Destroyer	$31-38	$63-75	$125-150
Talent and Booking	$9-10	$18-20	$35-40
The Originals (may not exist)	$20-25	$40-50	$80-100
Rock And Roll Over	$38-44	$75-88	$150-175
Love Gun	$31-38	$63-75	$125-150
The Land Of Hype And Glory	$6-8	$13-15	$25-30
Alive II	$31-38	$63-75	$125-150
Return To Casablanca	$9-10	$18-20	$35-40
Double Platinum	$13-19	$25-38	$50-75

Promotional Clear Elder poster. Jeff Barre collection.

Item	VG	EX	NM
Solo Albums (one kit)	$13-19	$25-38	$50-75
Dynasty	$10-13	$20-25	$40-50
Unmasked	$10-13	$20-25	$40-50
(Music From) The Elder	$10-13	$20-25	$40-50
Creatures of the Night	$10-13	$20-25	$40-50
Lick It Up	$4-5	$8-10	$15-20
Animalize	$3-4	$6-8	$12-15
Asylum	$3-4	$6-8	$12-15
Crazy Nights	$3-4	$6-8	$12-15
Smashes, Thrashes, & Hits	$3-4	$6-8	$12-15
Hot In The Shade	$3-4	$6-8	$12-15
Revenge	$3-4	$6-8	$12-15

Love Gun press kit.

Return to Casablanca press kit.

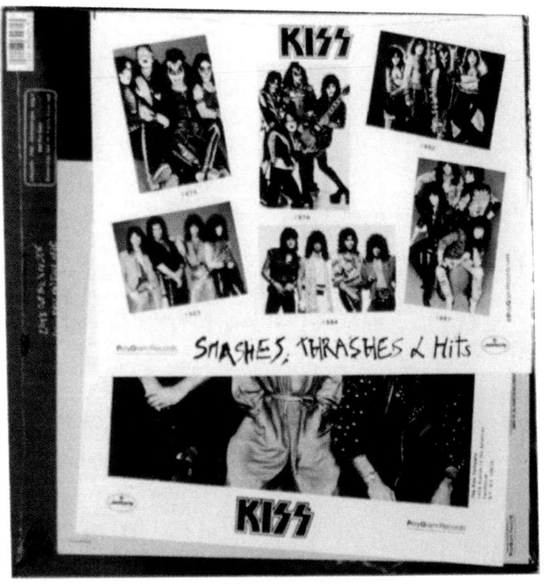

Promo Smashes Thrashes and Hits LP with press kit. Jeff Barre collection.

Psycho Circus Official Merchandise magazine.

A promotional Gibson counter display.

Paul Stanley Washburn Guitars, life-size standee.

A KISS on Sale end cap display. Jeff Barre collection.

Item	VG	EX	NM
Alive III	$3-4	$6-8	$12-15
Marvel Comics "KISS Classics"	$6-8	$13-15	$25-30
Official KISS Conventions	$6-8	$13-15	$25-30
MTV Unplugged	$4-5	$8-10	$15-20
You Wanted The Best...	$4-5	$8-10	$15-20
Reunion tour, black box	$38-50	$75-100	$150-200
Greatest KISS	$4-5	$8-10	$15-20
Psycho Circus	$31-38	$63-75	$125-150

Item	VG	EX	NM
The Box set	$0-0	$0-0	$0-0
(No official kits produced, promotion was done electronically)			
Promotional, retail order sheets/flyers			
Greatest KISS, phone card ad sheet	$1-2	$3-4	$5-8
KISS boot Green 4 x 6 ad	$0-1	$1-2	$1-3
KISS Visa application, 1997	$0-1	$1-2	$1-3
Majik Market cup sheet, with coupons on back	$6-8	$13-15	$25-30
Makeup sales flyer, Paper Magic	$1-2	$3-4	$5-8
Mask sales flyer, Paper Magic	$1-2	$3-4	$5-8
Psycho Circus Merchandise Mag	$0-1	$1-2	$1-3
Phone card/pick postcard order	$0-1	$1-2	$1-3
Phone card, four-page order sheet	$0-1	$1-2	$1-3
Punisher bass brochure	$1-1	$2-3	$3-5
Promotional, standees			
Ace Frehley, Gibson Guitars			
Life size	$63-75	$125-150	$250-300
Life size on tri-pole	$38-44	$75-88	$150-175
Counter display	$8-10	$15-20	$30-40
Paul Stanley, Silvertone, life size	$10-13	$20-25	$40-50
Paul Stanley, Washburn, life size	$15-19	$30-38	$60-75
Paul Stanley, Washburn, table top	$6-9	$13-18	$25-35
Peter Criss, Ahead, pad holder	$3-4	$6-8	$12-15
Gene Simmons AX, table top	$6-9	$13-18	$25-35
KISS Years store counter display	$3-4	$6-8	$12-15
Love Gun, 1977	$50-63	$100-125	$200-250
Love Gun, 1996	$63-75	$125-150	$250-300

A promotional Love Gun standee. Rich Vanderwerken collection.

Promotional mobile, Reunion Tour logo. Jeff Barre collection.

Item	VG	EX	NM
Telephone counter display	$8-10	$15-20	$30-40
24-inch dolls counter display	$6-9	$13-18	$25-35
Window stickers, Carnival of Souls	$1-2	$3-4	$5-8

Radio

Item	VG	EX	NM
AM transistor radio			
Boxed	$31-38	$63-75	$125-150
Loose	$19-25	$38-50	$75-100
Retail sales display box	$25-31	$50-63	$100-125
FM auto scan radio, sealed, 1998	$3-4	$6-8	$12-15

A 1977 AM radio, top, and a 1998 FM radio.

Item	VG	EX	NM

Record Awards, RIAA (chronological)

Awards issued to inner circle members of KISS are worth at least 150% of C9 value.

None of the first four albums (KISS, Hotter Than Hell, Dressed To Kill, Alive!) has ever been recognized by the recording Industry Association of America (RIAA) for sales beyond 1,000,000 units. Any Platinum awards for those albums are at best in-house awards, and are not official RIAA awards. At worst they are counterfeits.

Item	VG	EX	NM
KISS			
Gold	$225-300	$450-600	$900-1,200
Hotter Than Hell			
Gold	$225-300	$450-600	$900-1,200
Dressed To Kill			
Gold	$225-300	$450-600	$900-1,200
Alive!			
Gold	$225-300	$450-600	$900-1,200
Destroyer			
Gold	$225-300	$450-600	$900-1,200
Platinum	$225-300	$450-600	$900-1,200
Rock and Roll Over			
Gold	$225-300	$450-600	$900-1,200
Platinum	$225-300	$450-600	$900-1,200
Love Gun			
Gold	$225-300	$450-600	$900-1,200
Platinum	$225-300	$450-600	$900-1,200
Alive II			
Gold	$225-300	$450-600	$900-1,200

Item	VG	EX	NM
Platinum	$225-300	$450-600	$900-1,200
Double Platinum	$225-300	$450-600	$900-1,200
Double Platinum			
Gold	$225-300	$450-600	$900-1,200
Platinum	$225-300	$450-600	$900-1,200

Record player, Tiger

Boxed	$600-625	$1,200-1,250	$2,400-2,500
Loose	$125-150	$250-300	$500-600
Box only	$75-100	$150-200	$300-400

Tiger record player. Rich Vanderwerken collection.

Item	VG	EX	NM
Robe			
Black w/white saw blade logo	$16-18	$33-35	$65-70
Black w/tiger pelt collar, Psycho Circus logo	$16-18	$33-35	$65-70
Scarves			
Animalize, black with yellow and red logos	$4-5	$8-10	$15-20
Animalize, white, red, and blue	$4-5	$8-10	$15-20
Lick It Up, photos w/logo	$3-4	$6-8	$12-15
Black with logo and tassels	$13-19	$25-38	$50-75
Unmasked, each member, logo and Army emblem	$4-5	$8-10	$15-20
World Tour 1983-1984	$4-5	$8-10	$15-20
World Tour 1984, red, black, and gold	$4-5	$8-10	$15-20
Scream machine, Pepsi			
Blue	$31-38	$63-75	$125-150
Green	$31-38	$63-75	$125-150
Orange	$38-44	$75-88	$150-175
White	$31-38	$63-75	$125-150
Yellow	$13-19	$25-38	$50-75

A black scarf with logo and tassels. Rich Vanderwerken collection.

Pepsi Scream Machine, yellow.

Item	VG	EX	NM
Script (not photo copied)			
Phantom of the Park	$50-63	$100-125	$200-250
Millennium, TV show	$25-38	$50-75	$100-150
Mad TV	$25-38	$50-75	$100-150
Shirts			
Children's shirts			
Alive II button up, 1978 Sears	$25-31	$50-63	$100-125
Ace Frehley, 1978 Sears	$25-31	$50-63	$100-125
Button up "autograph" shirt			
With collar	$38-44	$75-88	$150-175
No collar	$38-44	$75-88	$150-175
Blue button up, faces "silk" shirt	$38-50	$75-100	$150-200
Brown, faces, "silk" shirt, pull over	$38-50	$75-100	$150-200
Dragonfly party/bowling shirt			
KISS Logo	$9-10	$18-20	$35-40
Love Gun	$9-10	$18-20	$35-40
Solo Faces	$9-10	$18-20	$35-40
Farewell Tour	$8-9	$15-18	$30-35
Sweatshirt			
KISS On Line	$5-6	$10-13	$20-25
Glow in dark faces	$5-6	$10-13	$20-25
T-shirts (all shirts assumed black unless noted)			
Ace Frehley			
Solo	$6-8	$13-15	$25-30
Full body, Farewell Tour	$4-5	$9-10	$17-20
Gibson guitar promo	$9-11	$18-23	$35-45

Item	VG	EX	NM
Peter Criss			
Solo	$6-8	$13-15	$25-30
Full body, Farewell Tour	$4-5	$9-10	$17-20
Paul Stanley			
Solo	$6-8	$13-15	$25-30
Full body, Farewell Tour	$4-5	$9-10	$17-20
Washburn, Black Diamond promo	$4-5	$8-9	$15-18
Gene Simmons			
Solo	$6-8	$13-15	$25-30
Full body, Farewell Tour	$4-5	$9-10	$17-20
RARO face, women's	$4-5	$9-10	$17-20

A promotional box set T-shirt.

Item	VG	EX	NM
Group			
3-D Live	$3-3	$5-6	$10-12
Alive II, on tan	$6-8	$13-15	$25-30
Alive II, on yellow	$6-8	$13-15	$25-30
Alive II US tour, on tan	$11-14	$23-28	$45-55
Alive III, Kiss Army on back	$4-5	$8-10	$15-20
Alive IV	$4-5	$8-9	$15-18
Alive/Worldwide tour local crew	$4-5	$8-10	$15-20
Alive/Worldwide tour crew	$9-13	$18-25	$35-50
Asylum, "World Tour 85-86"	$3-4	$6-8	$12-15
Box set (originally a promo item)	$4-5	$8-10	$15-20
Calling Dr. Love	$4-5	$8-10	$15-20
Crazy Nights, "I Went Crazy"	$3-4	$6-8	$12-15
Critics Quote, Farewell Tour	$4-5	$9-10	$17-20
Destroyer, Kiss Army on back	$3-4	$6-8	$12-15
Destroyer, on black	$4-5	$8-10	$15-20
Destroyer, cities on back, white shirt w/blue sleeves	$9-10	$18-20	$35-40
Destroyer, globe with 25 cities	$6-8	$13-15	$25-30
Destroyer, tie-dye	$6-8	$13-15	$25-30
Detroit Rock City (movie)	$3-3	$5-6	$10-12
Double Platinum	$11-14	$23-28	$45-55
Dynasty cover	$9-11	$18-23	$35-45
Dynasty cover, on tan	$9-11	$18-23	$35-45
Dynasty, Return of Kiss on back	$9-11	$18-23	$35-45
Dynasty World Tour 1979	$9-11	$18-23	$35-45
Four Who are One	$3-3	$5-6	$10-12

Item	VG	EX	NM
Four Who are One with stars	$3-3	$5-6	$10-12
Green 1976 Photo, glow in dark	$3-3	$5-6	$10-12
KISS Army, green, 1996	$4-5	$8-10	$15-20
KISS Army, XXL Defense Dept.	$4-5	$8-10	$15-20
KISS 1st LP cover	$4-5	$8-10	$15-20
KISS Exposed, promo white tank	$9-10	$18-20	$35-40
KISS My Ass, title on back	$4-5	$8-10	$15-20
KISS On Line	$4-5	$9-10	$17-20
KISSopoly	$1-1	$2-3	$3-5
KISS Rock And Rule The World	$4-5	$9-10	$17-20
KISS 2000	$4-5	$8-9	$15-18
Legends Never Die, Farewell	$4-5	$9-10	$17-20
Local Crew (assorted tours)	$9-10	$18-20	$35-40
Logo with faces from 1979	$6-8	$13-15	$25-30
Logo with solo faces, tie-dye	$6-8	$13-15	$25-30
Logo with solo faces, long-sleeve tie-dye	$6-8	$13-15	$25-30
Logo in Rhinestones	$5-6	$10-13	$20-25
Love Gun, on tan	$6-8	$13-15	$25-30
Matt Crafton NASCAR Truck series	$6-8	$13-15	$25-30
Merry KISSmas	$4-5	$8-10	$15-20
Metallic logo	$6-8	$13-15	$25-30
Musical touch pad, plays Rock And Roll All Nite	$5-6	$10-13	$20-25
Not Dead Yet	$4-5	$8-10	$15-20
The Originals w/album covers	$3-3	$5-6	$10-12
Post card, KISS 2000	$4-5	$8-10	$15-20
Psycho As Hell	$3-3	$5-6	$10-12

Local crew concert shirts.

Item	VG	EX	NM
Psycho Cage	$3-3	$5-6	$10-12
Psycho Circus, tie-dye	$3-3	$5-6	$10-12
Psycho Faces in frames	$3-3	$5-6	$10-12
Psycho KISSmas, straight jackets	$3-3	$5-6	$10-12
Psycho Wagon, tie-dye	$3-3	$5-6	$10-12
Psycho Motorcycles	$3-3	$5-6	$10-12
Revenge, red logo with skulls	$4-5	$8-10	$15-20
Revenge, Revenge in blood	$4-5	$8-10	$15-20
Rock And Roll Over, tie-dye	$6-8	$13-15	$25-30
Santa Swami KISSmas	$3-3	$5-6	$10-12
Solo Art work combined	$6-8	$13-15	$25-30
Unholy, skull front, logo back	$4-5	$8-10	$15-20
Unplugged	$4-5	$8-10	$15-20
WCW Event	$4-4	$8-9	$15-17
Welcome to the Psycho Circus	$3-3	$5-6	$10-12
World tour 1979, long sleeve	$9-11	$18-23	$35-45
World tour 1979	$9-11	$18-23	$35-45
World tour 1979, tan	$9-11	$18-23	$35-45
World tour 1979, security	$13-15	$25-30	$50-60
Y2 KISS	$4-4	$8-9	$15-17
You Wanted the Best, tie-dye	$6-8	$13-15	$25-30

Shoelaces

Item	VG	EX	NM
Red logos			
On card	$31-38	$63-75	$125-150
Loose	$13-19	$25-38	$50-75

Shoelaces: faces, left, and red logos.
Rich Vanderwerken collection.

Item	VG	EX	NM
Faces			
On card	$31-38	$63-75	$125-150
Loose	$13-19	$25-38	$50-75

Skateboard

With wheels, or trucks	$30-34	$60-68	$120-135
Without wheels, or trucks	$15-18	$30-35	$60-70

Sleeping bag

In package	$169-175	$338-350	$675-700
Loose	$88-100	$175-200	$350-400

Slippers

Demon shoe	$13-15	$25-30	$50-60
Psycho Circus, Ace Frehley, Peter Criss, Paul Stanley or Gene Simmons	$6-8	$13-15	$25-30

Snow globes

Each member, boxed	$3-4	$6-8	$12-15
Group with logo in globe, boxed	$6-8	$13-15	$25-30
Iceman Guitar with logo	$13-15	$25-30	$50-60

Sleeping bag. Rich Vanderwerken collection.

Demon slippers.

Snow Globe, with logo in globe.

Iceman guitar snow globe.

Gene Simmons Destroyer statue.

Item	VG	EX	NM
Statues			
Gene Simmons Destroyer	$8-9	$15-18	$30-35

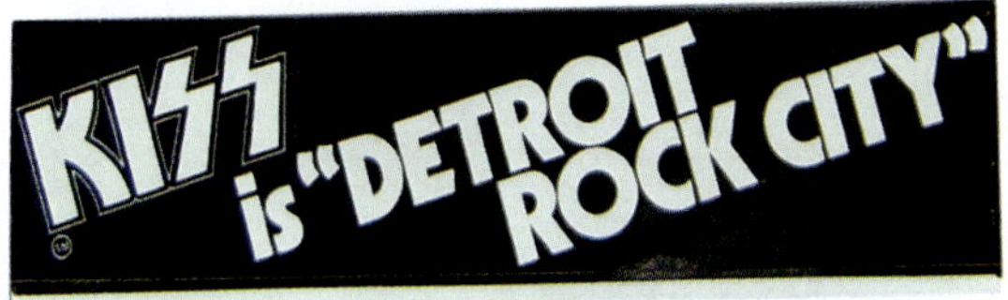

Detroit Rock City sticker.

Item	VG	EX	NM
Stickers			
Stickers, bumper			
Animalize, logo and group photo	$1-1	$2-3	$3-5
Blazefest	$2-3	$5-6	$9-12
Detroit Rock City	$0-1	$1-2	$1-3
Faces in logo	$0-1	$1-2	$1-3
Faces with flames	$0-1	$1-2	$1-3
KISS is Detroit Rock City	$6-8	$13-15	$25-30
KISS my ass	$0-1	$1-2	$1-3
KISS This, set of two	$0-1	$1-2	$1-3
Red logo	$0-1	$1-2	$1-3
Stickers, puffy			
Booklet	$56-63	$113-125	$225-250
Set of four, sealed	$25-30	$50-60	$100-120
Set of four, unsealed	$15-20	$30-40	$60-80
Each, sealed	$6-8	$13-15	$25-30
Each, unsealed	$4-5	$8-10	$15-20
Australian, sealed	$31-38	$63-75	$125-150

Stickers, wall border, faces in logo, left, and solo faces.

Item	VG	EX	NM
Australian, unsealed	$19-25	$38-50	$75-100
Sticker, wall border			
Solo faces border	$3-4	$6-8	$12-15
Faces in logo border	$3-4	$6-8	$12-15

Item	VG	EX	NM
Four pack on large card	$4-5	$8-10	$15-20
Sticker, window, static cling			
Destroyer	$1-1	$1-3	$2-5
Not Dead Yet	$1-1	$1-3	$2-5
Rock and Roll Over	$1-1	$1-3	$2-5

Telephone

Round, Destroyer artwork			
Boxed	$6-8	$13-15	$25-30
Loose	$3-4	$6-8	$12-15

Telephone, Destroyer artwork.

Item	VG	EX	NM
Tickets			
1973			
Full	$138-150	$275-300	$550-600
Stub	$38-44	$75-88	$150-175
1974			
Full	$25-31	$50-63	$100-125
Stub	$13-15	$25-30	$50-60
1975			
Full	$13-15	$25-30	$50-60
Stub	$4-5	$8-10	$15-20
1976			
Full	$13-15	$25-30	$50-60
Stub	$4-5	$8-10	$15-20
1977-1983			
Full	$9-10	$18-20	$35-40
Stub	$2-3	$4-5	$7-10
1984-1995			
Full	$2-3	$4-5	$7-10
Stub	$1-2	$2-3	$3-6
1996-present			
Full	$2-3	$4-5	$7-10
Stub	$1-2	$2-3	$3-6
KISS Meets The Phantom concert, 1978			
Red admission			
Full	$81-88	$163-175	$325-350
Stub	$10-13	$20-25	$40-50

Ticket, Aug. 10, 1973 (reproduction).

Ticket, Argentina, 1997.

Item	VG	EX	NM
Green press pass			
Full	$81-88	$163-175	$325-350
Stub	$10-13	$20-25	$40-50
Parking pass			
Full	$10-13	$20-25	$40-50
Stub	$5-8	$10-15	$20-30
MTV Unplugged, 1995			
Full	$13-19	$25-38	$50-75
Stub	$5-6	$10-13	$20-25

Ties

Album covers	$2-2	$3-5	$6-9
First LP pose	$2-2	$3-5	$6-9
Psycho Circus faces	$2-2	$3-5	$6-9
Reunion faces	$2-2	$3-5	$6-9
Solo faces	$2-2	$3-5	$6-9
Solo faces on logos	$2-2	$3-5	$6-9
Solo faces with signatures	$2-2	$3-5	$6-9

An assortment of ties, from left: album covers, solo faces with signatures, reunion faces, and first LP pose.

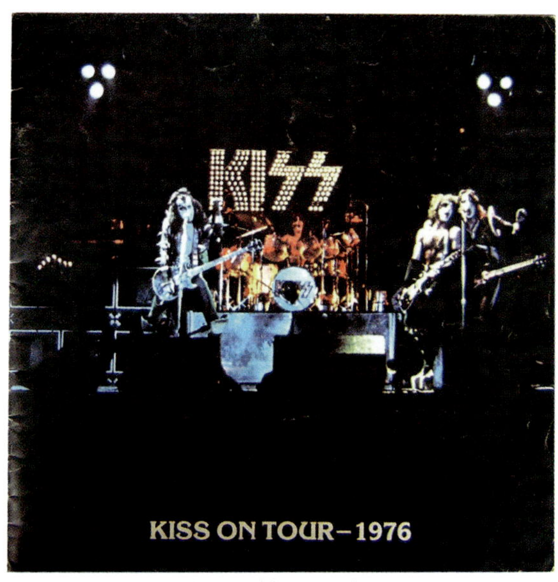

KISS on Tour-1976 (ALIVE! Tour) program.

Item	VG	EX	NM
Tour programs/tour books (chronological)			
Prices assume all inserts are intact.			
KISS On Tour-1976 (ALIVE! Tour)	$81-88	$163-175	$325-350

Item	VG	EX	NM
On Tour (Destroyer tour)	$38-44	$75-88	$150-175
On Tour (Rock and Roll Over)	$29-33	$58-65	$115-130
World Tour '77 &'78 (Love Gun/ Alive II/Double Platinum)	$15-19	$30-38	$60-75
Japan 1977 (Rock and Roll Over)	$44-50	$88-100	$175-200
Japan 1978 (Love Gun Tour)	$44-50	$88-100	$175-200
The Return of KISS (Alternate Dynasty Tour book)	$300-375	$600-750	$1,200-1,500
Dynasty Tour (Gene ad)	$9-13	$18-25	$35-50
Dynasty Tour (Paul ad)	$15-19	$30-38	$60-75
Unmasked Tour (Europe)	$38-44	$75-88	$150-175
Unmasked Tour, censored logo (Germany)	$38-44	$75-88	$150-175
Unmasked Tour (Australia)	$38-44	$75-88	$150-175
10th anniversary tour (Creatures)	$44-50	$88-100	$175-200
World Tour 1983-84 (Lick It Up tour Europe)	$13-16	$25-33	$50-65
World Tour 1984 (Lick It Up tour, America)	$8-10	$15-20	$30-40
World Tour 1984-85 (Animalize tour)			
Mark St. John cover	$8-10	$15-20	$30-40
Bruce Kulick cover	$8-10	$15-20	$30-40
Asylum Tour	$11-13	$23-25	$45-50
Crazy Nights World Tour, 1987-88	$10-13	$20-25	$40-50
Monsters of Rock 1988	$13-16	$25-33	$50-65
Crazy Nights Tour (Japan)	$20-25	$40-50	$80-100
Hot in the Shade World Tour	$9-11	$18-23	$35-45

KISS on Tour-1976 (ALIVE! Tour) tour program merchandise insert.

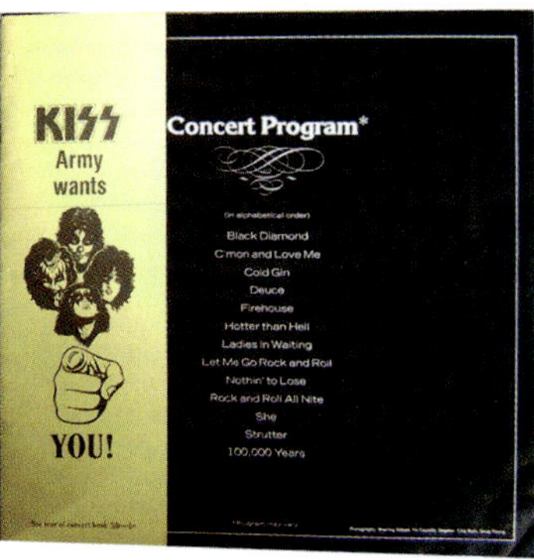

On-Tour program, Destroyer and Rock and Roll Over tours.

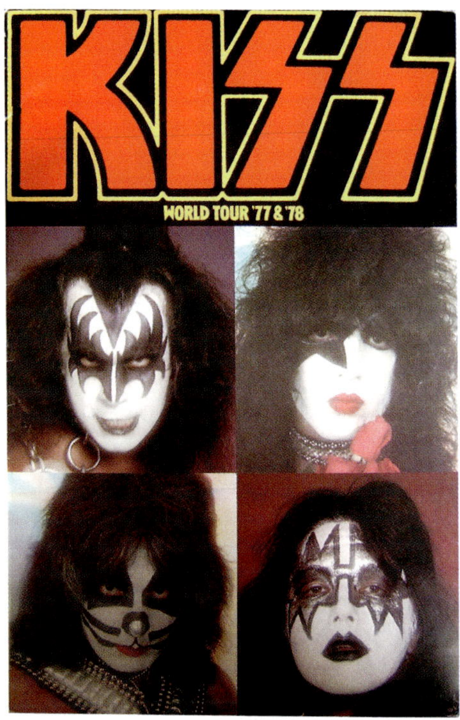

World Tour '77 and '78 tour program, Love Gun and Alive II tours.

The 1977-78 World Tour program, from Japan.

Dynasty Tour program (The Return of KISS).

Unmasked Tour program (Australia).

Animalize 1984-85 World Tour program, Mark St. John cover.

Item	VG	EX	NM
Revenge	$31-38	$63-75	$125-150
Blazefest	$5-6	$10-13	$20-25
KISS convention, Australia 1995	$4-5	$8-10	$15-20
KISS convention, America 1995	$4-5	$8-10	$15-20
Weenie Roast, 1996	$4-5	$8-10	$15-20
Alive/Worldwide 96-97, version 1	$6-8	$13-15	$25-30
Monsters Of Rock 1996	$9-10	$18-20	$35-40
Alive/Worldwide 96-97, Japan	$5-6	$10-13	$20-25
Alive/Worldwide 96-97, version 2	$6-9	$13-18	$25-35

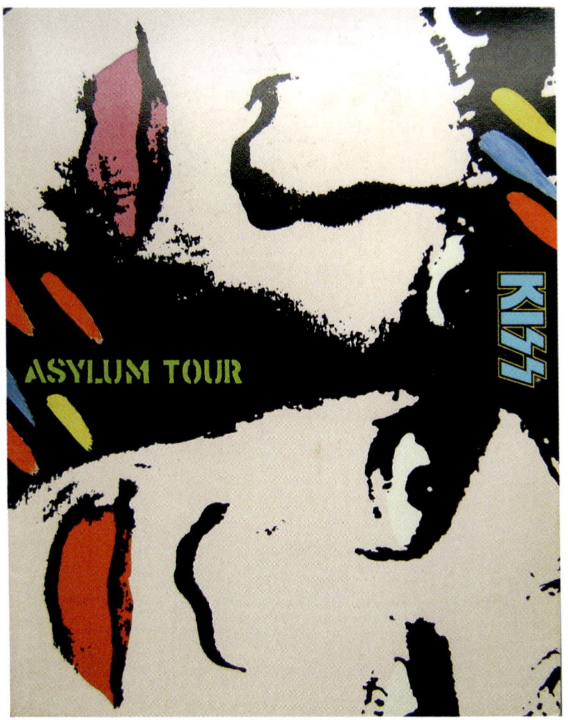

Asylum Tour program.

Alive Worldwide 1996-97 Tour program, Version 1, Version 2 and Japan.

Alive Worldwide 1996-97 Tour program, Europe, silver cover.

Alive Worldwide 1996-97 Tour program, Europe, retail reprint.

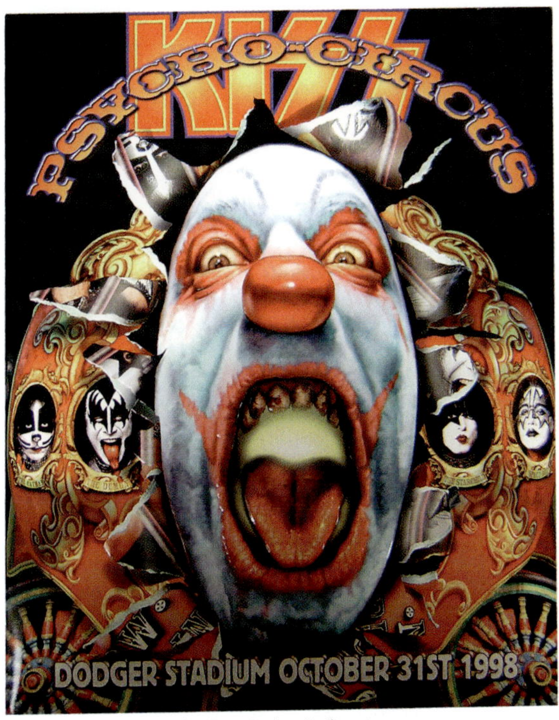

A Psycho Circus Dodger Stadium program.

A Psycho Circus World Tour 1998-1999 program.

A Farewell Tour program, USA.

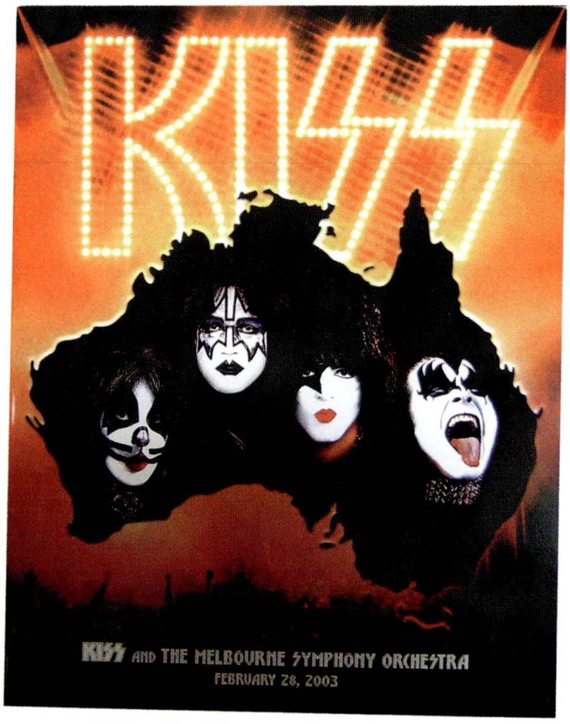

A KISS and the Melbourne Symphony Orchestra program.

Item	VG	EX	NM
Alive/Worldwide 96-97, Europe			
Silver cover	$6-8	$13-15	$25-30
Retail reprint	$2-3	$4-5	$7-10
Psycho Circus Tour			
Dodger Stadium, October 1998	$6-8	$13-15	$25-30
World Tour, 1998-1999	$5-6	$10-13	$20-25
Farewell Tour, USA	$5-6	$10-13	$20-25
Farewell Tour, Japan, with Eric Singer insert	$6-8	$13-15	$25-30
Farewell Tour, Australia, with Eric Singer insert	$6-8	$13-15	$25-30
KISS with Melbourne Symphony	$29-33	$58-65	$115-130
Japan, 2003	$20-25	$40-50	$80-100
World Domination	$2-3	$4-5	$7-10
Rock the Nation	$4-5	$8-10	$15-20

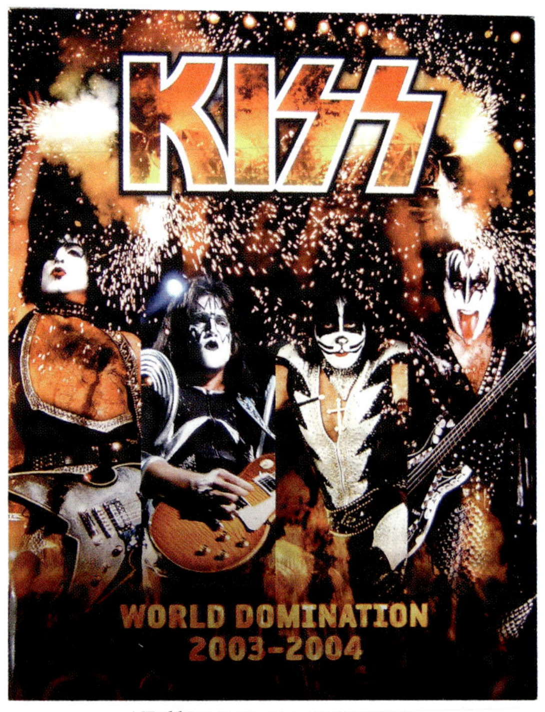

A World Domination Tour 2003 program.

Rock the Nation 2004 World Tour Program.

An inside back-cover page of the Australian version of the Rock the Nation Tour Program on P. 337.

Item	VG	EX	NM
Towels, beach			
Faces and logo	$38-44	$75-88	$150-175
Group on cubes	$38-44	$75-88	$150-175
Australian	$44-50	$88-100	$175-200
Trash can	$75-81	$150-163	$300-325
Umbrella			
Rock and Roll Over	$13-15	$25-30	$50-60
Solo faces	$13-15	$25-30	$50-60
Underoos			
Gene RARO	$4-5	$8-10	$15-20
Love Gun	$4-5	$8-10	$15-20
Van, radio control			
Boxed, flap style	$600-625	$1,200-1,250	$2,400-2,500
Boxed, no flap style	$500-575	$1,000-1,150	$2,000-2,300
Van and controller, loose	$63-75	$125-150	$250-300
Van only, loose	$19-25	$38-50	$75-100
View-Master			
Reels in sleeve	$9-11	$18-23	$35-45
Reels loose	$1-2	$3-4	$5-8
Reels in sleeve, with two other sets	$9-13	$18-25	$35-50

Beach towel, faces and logo, Rich Vanderwerken collection.

Both sides of the KISS trash can.

View-Master, sleeves loose.

Item	VG	EX	NM
Videotapes, official			
Animalized Live Uncensored	$5-6	$10-13	$20-25
Detroit Rock City	$3-4	$6-8	$12-15
Crazy Nights	$4-5	$8-10	$15-20
Inside The Casaba	$4-5	$8-10	$15-20
KISS Exposed	$4-5	$8-10	$15-20

"The Second Coming" videotape and DVD.

Item	VG	EX	NM
KISS Konfidential	$4-5	$8-10	$15-20
KISS Meets The Phantom			
Clamshell case	$9-13	$18-25	$35-50
Slipcase	$4-5	$8-10	$15-20
KISS My ASS	$4-5	$8-10	$15-20
KISS X-treme Closeup	$4-5	$8-10	$15-20
MTV Unplugged	$4-5	$8-10	$15-20
Psycho Circus, with glasses and member picture CD			
Ace Frehley, Peter Criss, Paul Stanley or Gene Simmons CD	$3-4	$5-8	$10-15
CD in package backwards	$4-5	$8-10	$15-20
The Second Coming	$6-8	$13-15	$25-30

Wine

Item	VG	EX	NM
Destroyer label, alcoholic			
Sealed	$11-13	$23-25	$45-50
Open	$4-5	$8-10	$15-20
Etched Destroyer, alcoholic			
Sealed	$15-16	$30-33	$60-65
Open	$4-5	$8-10	$15-20
Solo faces label, non-alcoholic			
Sealed	$11-13	$23-25	$45-50
Open	$4-5	$8-10	$15-20
Etched faces, non-alcoholic			
Ace Frehley, Peter Criss, Paul Stanley or Gene Simmons			
Sealed	$15-16	$30-33	$60-65
Open	$4-5	$8-10	$15-20

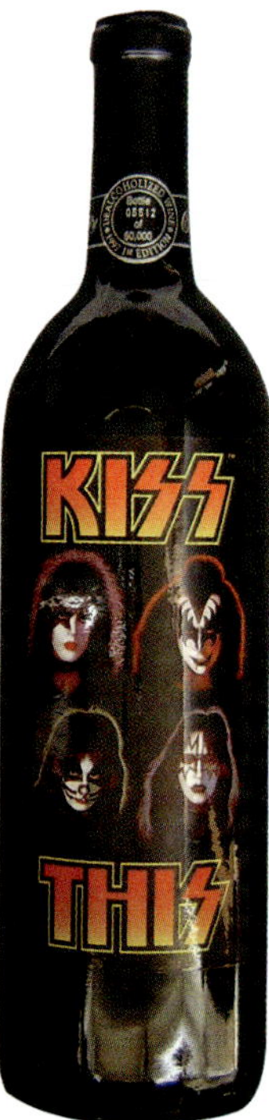

Wine, Solo faces label, non-alcoholic.

Item	VG	EX	NM
Wristband			
Cotton sweatbands			
Solo faces, each	$1-1	$2-3	$3-5
Logo	$1-1	$2-3	$3-5
Leather with logo			
Connected icons	$4-5	$8-9	$15-18
Separated icons	$5-6	$11-12	$21-24
Yo-Yo			
Psycho Circus Coin			
Each member			
Blue coin	$9-10	$18-20	$35-40
Gold plated blue coin	$14-15	$28-30	$55-60

American and selected foreign music (chronological)

Inserts are priced separate from their album. Add the values together to get a package value.

(Worldwide LP covers can be seen at www.kisshall.com)

Item	VG	EX	NM
Pre-KISS releases			
Peter Criss			
Chelsea	$19-25	$38-50	$75-100
Paul Stanley, Gene Simmons			
Lyn Christopher	$25-31	$50-63	$100-125

Hard Goods. This Warner Brothers' sampler was most likely the first appearance of KISS on vinyl.

From the Casbah, featuring three KISS tracks from Dressed to Kill.

Item	VG	EX	NM
Promo-only (all are LPs unless listed otherwise)			
Hard Goods	$16-18	$33-35	$65-70
From the Casbah	$13-15	$25-30	$50-60
Special KISS Tour Album			
KISS '76 (USA, 1976)	$20-25	$40-50	$80-100
PSR-398 (UK, 1976)	$19-20	$38-40	$75-80
Rock and Roll Over Special Edition,			
NBLP-737 (USA, 1976)	$44-50	$88-100	$175-200
Return To Casablanca	$11-13	$23-25	$45-50
Return To Casablanca Vol. II			
LPs	$11-13	$23-25	$45-50
8-track	$11-13	$23-25	$45-50
Cassette	$11-13	$23-25	$45-50
Casablanca Fair (Japan)	$56-63	$113-125	$225-250
A Taste of Platinum NBD 20128 (USA, 1978)	$31-38	$63-75	$125-150
The KISS Albums (Black box, or KISS Bible)	$25-31	$50-63	$100-125
Cassettes (no release code) (USA, 1978)			
Peter Criss, Ace Frehley, Gene Simmons, Paul Stanley assembled especially for Radio			
NBD 20137 DJ (USA, 1978)	$9-10	$18-20	$35-40
Hot Hits To Warm Your Winter			
SA 054 (USA, 1984)	$8-9	$15-18	$30-35
First KISS...Last Licks			
PRO 792-1 (USA, 1990)	$20-25	$40-50	$80-100
Universal Presents Gimme KISS, cassettes			
SAC-175 (USA, 1990)	$9-10	$18-20	$35-40

Return to Casablanca, Volume II.

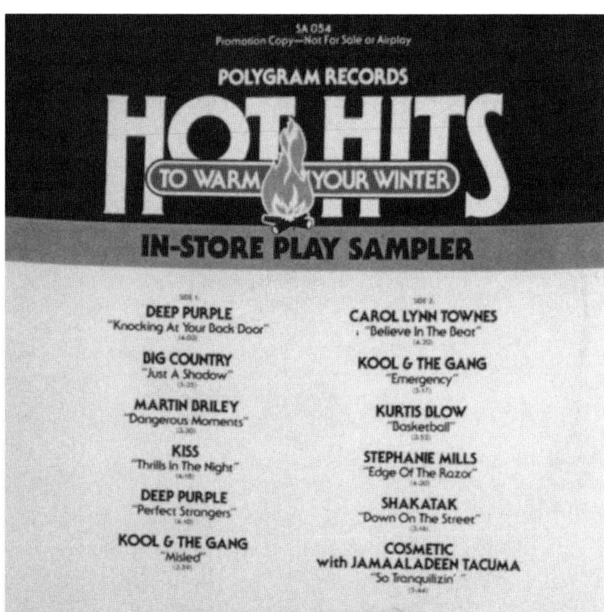

Hot Hits to Warm Your Winter. Jeff Barre Collection.

Universal Presents Gimme KISS.

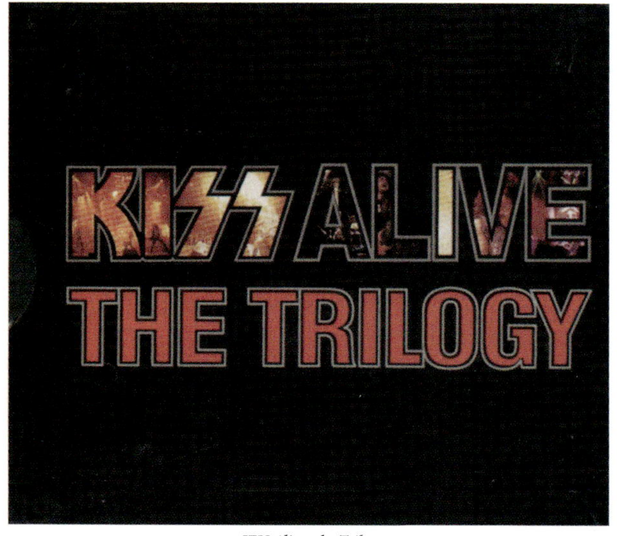

KISS Alive, the Trilogy.

Promo advance sampler for the KISS box set, Canada.

Item	VG	EX	NM
Killer Cuts From Revenge, cassettes			
SAC-509 (USA, 1992)	$9-10	$18-20	$35-40
KISS Alive The Trilogy, CDs			
KISS SLIPCASE-1 (USA, 1993)	$25-30	$50-63	$100-125
Box set sampler, CDs			
UMCF-4602-2 (Canada, 2001)	$50-63	$100-125	$200-250
USA promo 12" singles			
I Was Made For Lovin' You			
NBD 20169 DJ, 1979	$5-6	$10-13	$20-25
Lick It Up			
PRO 229-1, 1983	$4-5	$8-10	$15-20
All Hell's Breaking Lose			
PRO 244-1, 1983	$4-5	$8-10	$15-20
Heavens on Fire			
PRO 311-1, 1984	$4-5	$8-10	$15-20
Thrills in the Night			
PRO 326-1, 1984	$4-5	$8-10	$15-20
Tears Are Falling			
PRO 377-1, 1985	$4-5	$8-10	$15-20
UH! All Night			
PRO 395-1, 1985	$4-5	$8-10	$15-20
Crazy, Crazy Nights			
PRO 531-1, 1987	$4-5	$8-10	$15-20
Reason to Live			
PRO 559-1, 1987	$4-5	$8-10	$15-20

Item	VG	EX	NM
Turn on the Night			
PRO 572-1, 1987	$4-5	$8-10	$15-20
Let's Put the X in Sex (3 mixes)/Calling Dr Love			
PRO 693, 1989	$31-38	$63-75	$125-150
Foreign 12" Singles			
Hard Luck Woman/Calling Dr. Love/Beth			
UK CANL-102	$4-5	$8-10	$15-20
Rocket Ride/Shock Me			
UK CANL-117	$4-5	$8-10	$15-20
I Was Made For Lovin' You/Hard Times			
UK CANL-152	$4-5	$8-10	$15-20
France			
Blue vinyl	$9-10	$18-20	$35-40
Red vinyl	$9-10	$18-20	$35-40
Yellow vinyl	$9-10	$18-20	$35-40
Mexico			
Yellow vinyl	$10-13	$20-25	$40-50
Green vinyl	$10-13	$20-25	$40-50
2,000 Man/I Was Made For Lovin' You/Sure Know Something			
UK NBL-1001	$4-5	$8-10	$15-20
Killer/I Love It Loud/I Was Made For Lovin' You			
UK KISS-312, pic sleeve	$4-5	$8-10	$15-20
Creatures of the Night/Rock and Roll All Nite			
UK KISD-4 (Double groove A side, autographed B-side)	$9-10	$18-20	$35-40

I Was Made For Lovin' You, 12-inch single, yellow, Mexico.

Creatures of the Night, UK KISD-4, double-grooved.

Item	VG	EX	NM
Creatures of the Night/War Machine/Rock and Roll All Nite (Live)			
UK KISS-412, pic sleeve	$4-5	$8-10	$15-20
Lick It Up/Not for the Innocent/I Still Love You			
UK KISS-512, pic sleeve	$4-5	$8-10	$15-20
Heaven's On Fire/Lonely Is The Hunter/All Hell's Breakin' Loose			
UK VERX-12, poster, pic sleeve	$4-5	$8-10	$15-20
Tears Are Falling/Heaven's On Fire (Live)/Any Way You Slice It			
UK KIZZ-A1, Promo	$6-8	$13-15	$25-30
Tears Are Falling Heaven's On Fire (Live)/Any Way You Slice It			
UK KISS-612, sticker, pic sleeve	$4-5	$8-10	$15-20
Crazy Crazy Nights/No, No, No/Lick It Up/Uh! All Nite			
UK KISS-712, pic sleeve	$4-5	$8-10	$15-20
Reason to Live/Thief in the Night/Who Wants to Be Lonely/Thrills in the Night			
UK KISS-812, pic sleeve	$4-5	$8-10	$15-20
Turn on the Night/Hell or High Water/King of the Mountain/ Any Way You Slice It	$4-5	$8-10	$15-20
Let's Put the X in Sex/Rock and Roll All Nite/Heaven's on Fire/Lick It Up			
UK KIZZ-A2, promo	$6-8	$13-15	$25-30
Hide Your Heart/Betrayed/Boomerang			
UK KISX-10, pic sleeve	$4-5	$8-10	$15-20
Forever (Remix)/All American Man/Shandi/The Oath			
UK KISX-11, pic sleeve	$4-5	$8-10	$15-20
Forever (Remix)/The Street Giveth.../Deuce ('73 Demo)/Strutter ('73 Demo)			
UK KISGX-11, pic sleeve	$6-9	$13-18	$25-35
God Gave Rock and Roll to You II (Edit)/(Album)			
UK A8696-12, pic sleeve	$4-5	$8-10	$15-20

Item	VG	EX	NM
Unholy/Partners In Crime (Remix)/Deuce ('73 Demo)/Strutter ('73 Demo)			
UK KISS-1212, white vinyl	$6-9	$13-18	$25-35
Promo CD singles (USA unless noted)			
Strutter + 2 (Austrian bootleg, set of five 3" CDs)	$6-8	$13-15	$25-30
Crazy, Crazy Nights			
CDP-4, 1987	$3-4	$6-8	$12-15
Let's Put the X in Sex			
CDP-35, 1988	$4-5	$8-10	$15-20
Hide Your Heart			
CDP-140, 1989	$3-4	$6-8	$12-15
Forever (remix)			
CDP-195, 1989	$3-4	$6-8	$12-15
Rise to It (radio edit)/(full power guitar mix)			
CDP-242, 1990	$3-4	$6-8	$12-15
God Gave Rock and Roll to You (edit)/(album version)			
PRCD 4076 picture disc, 1991	$3-4	$6-8	$12-15
PRCD 4076 plain disc, 1991	$3-4	$6-8	$12-15
Unholy + 3			
CDP-666, 1992	$3-4	$6-8	$12-15
Domino (radio eq)/(radio edit)			
CDP-681, 1992	$3-4	$6-8	$12-15
I Just Wanna (radio eq)/(radio edit)			
CDP-707, 1992	$3-4	$6-8	$12-15
Everytime I Look At You			
CDP-776, 1992	$3-4	$6-8	$12-15

Item	VG	EX	NM
I Love it Loud (live)			
CDP-882, 1993	$3-4	$6-8	$12-15
I Love it Loud + 3			
CDP-910, 1993	$3-4	$6-8	$12-15
Rock and Roll All Nite			
CDP-947, 1993	$3-4	$6-8	$12-15
Everytime I Look At You/Rock and Roll All Nite			
CDP-1579, 1996	$3-4	$6-8	$12-15
New York Groove (Live) (Blockbuster Music exclusive)			
MECP-120	$11-13	$23-25	$45-50
Jungle (radio edit)/(full version)			
MECP-279, 1997	$3-4	$6-8	$12-15
Master and Slave			
MECP-367, 1998	$3-4	$6-8	$12-15
Psycho Circus (edit)/(album version)			
MECP-434, 1998	$3-4	$6-8	$12-15
You Wanted the Best			
MECP-462, 1998	$3-4	$6-8	$12-15
Nothing Can Keep Me From You			
MECP-1024, 1999	$3-4	$6-8	$12-15

Radio shows

Nightbird & Company

Item	VG	EX	NM
Hosted by Allison Steel 6/23/74	$19-25	$38-50	$75-100
Hosted by Allison Steel 9/19/75	$19-25	$38-50	$75-100

Nightbird & Company radio show, June 23, 1974.

NIGHTBIRD & COMPANY

with ALISON STEELE
presented by the
UNITED STATES ARMY RESERVE

Compatible-stereo music and talk with today's top ROCK artists.

Program #161 – CHARLIE DANIELS	Air week of 6/2/74
Program #162 – LARRY CORYELL	Air week of 6/9/74
Program #163 – B. J. THOMAS	Air week of 6/16/74
Program #164 – KISS	Air week of 6/23/74

FOR 10:00 MINUTES:

FOR 15:00 MINUTES:

FOR 25:00 MINUTES:

Item	VG	EX	NM
Three Musical Biographies			
DWJ Associates, 1976	$19-25	$38-50	$75-100
Rock and Roll Over With KISS			
Burns Media Consultants, Inc.			
BMC-001A (USA, 1976)	$75-81	$150-163	$300-325
King Biscuit Flower Power Hour			
Best of the Biscuit			
KISS & Heaven (KISS recorded in Nashville, Jan. 1984)			
(USA, 1984)	$13-15	$25-30	$50-60
KISS & Motley Crue (KISS recorded in Nashville, Jan. 1984)			
(USA, 1984)	$13-15	$25-30	$50-60
KISS & Twisted Sister (KISS recorded in Nashville, Jan. 1984)			
(USA, 1985)	$13-15	$25-30	$50-60
Metalshop Show #52	$10-13	$20-25	$40-50
MS-52 (USA, 1985) Broadcast Jan. 25, 1985			
Metalshop Show #110	$10-13	$20-25	$40-50
MS-110 (USA, 1986) Hosted by Ronnie James Dio. Broadcast March 7, 1986			
Metal Mania With Gene Simmons of KISS			
DIR Broadcasting (USA, 1986)			
Broadcast March 23, 1986	$10-13	$20-25	$40-50

Rock and Roll Over with KISS, Burns Media. Jeff Barre Collection.

Item	VG	EX	NM
Albums			

(Albums and label variations can be seen at www.kisshall.com)

Every KISS album up to and including the 1996 title You Wanted The Best, You Got The Best was released on vinyl. Since that time, the only legitimate USA vinyl pressing was KISS Symphony Alive IV. The first five albums were pressed with Blue labels, and as a general rule, the earlier the pressing, the more valuable the recording. Here is a sampling of some of the band's albums and prices. All are printed in the USA, unless noted otherwise.

Item	VG	EX	NM
KISS			
LPs, NB-9001 (1974)			
Blue label	$13-19	$25-38	$50-75
Promotional	$44-50	$88-100	$175-200
Test press	$63-75	$125-150	$250-300
Acetate	$63-75	$125-150	$250-300
NBL7001 (1975)	$63-75	$125-150	$250-300
Blue label	$6-8	$13-15	$25-30
Camel label (1976)	$2-3	$5-6	$9-12
Filmworks label (1977)	$2-3	$5-6	$9-12
824-146-1 (1985)	$2-3	$5-6	$9-12
Hotter Than Hell			
LPs, NBLP-7006 (1974)			
Blue label	$6-8	$13-15	$25-30
Promotional	$15-19	$30-38	$60-75
Test pressing	$20-25	$40-50	$80-100

Item	VG	EX	NM
Acetate	$20-25	$40-50	$80-100
Camel label (1976)	$2-3	$5-6	$9-12
Filmworks label (1977)	$2-3	$5-6	$9-12
824-147-1 (1985)	$2-3	$5-6	$9-12
Dressed to Kill			
LPs, NBLP-7016 (1975)			
Blue label	$6-8	$13-15	$25-30
Promotional	$15-19	$30-38	$60-75
Test pressing	$20-25	$40-50	$80-100
Acetate	$20-25	$40-50	$80-100
Camel label (1976)	$2-3	$5-6	$9-12
Filmworks label (1977)	$2-3	$5-6	$9-12
824-148-1 (1985)	$2-3	$5-6	$9-12
Alive!			
LPs, USA, NBLP-7020 (1975)			
Blue label	$9-10	$18-20	$35-40
Promotional	$18-20	$35-40	$70-80
Test pressing	$50-56	$100-113	$200-225
Acetate	$20-25	$40-50	$80-100
Camel label (1976)	$3-4	$6-8	$12-15
Filmworks label (1977)	$3-4	$6-8	$12-15
822-780-1 (1985)	$4-5	$8-10	$15-20
Inserts			
Booklet	$2-3	$4-5	$8-10

Alive! LP, USA.

Item	VG	EX	NM
Argentina SEL-647, 1976	$20-25	$40-50	$80-100
Argentina SEL-648, 1976	$20-25	$40-50	$80-100
NBLP87020 (USA, 1975)	$4-5	$8-10	$15-20

Alive! part one, Argentina.

Alive!, part two, Argentina.

Item	VG	EX	NM
Destroyer			
LPs, NBLP-7025 (1976)			
Blue label	$6-8	$13-15	$25-30
Promotional	$13-19	$25-38	$50-75
Test pressing	$20-25	$40-50	$80-100
Acetate	$20-25	$40-50	$80-100
Camel label (1976)	$2-3	$5-6	$9-12
Filmworks label (1977)	$2-3	$5-6	$9-12
824-149-1 (1985)	$2-3	$5-6	$9-12
Reel-to-reel tape			
CAF 7025 (USA, 1976)	$9-13	$18-25	$35-50
The Originals			
LPs, USA, NBLP-7032 (1976)			
Camel label	$20-25	$40-50	$80-100
Promotional	$50-63	$100-125	$200-250
Test pressing	$63-75	$125-150	$250-300
Acetate	$25-31	$50-63	$100-125
Filmworks label (1977)	$16-18	$33-35	$65-70
Inserts			
Booklet	$3-4	$6-8	$12-15
Cards, uncut	$3-4	$6-8	$12-15
Cards, cut	$2-2	$3-5	$6-9
Army sticker	$4-5	$8-10	$15-20
Japan VIP-5501-3 color obi, 1977	$44-50	$88-100	$175-200

Destroyer, reel-to-reel tape.

The Originals, Japan.

Item	VG	EX	NM
Rock and Roll Over			
LPs, USA, NBLP-7037 (1976)			
Camel label	$5-6	$10-13	$20-25
Promotional	$9-10	$18-20	$35-40
Test pressing	$20-25	$40-50	$80-100
Acetate	$20-25	$40-50	$80-100
Filmworks label, 1977	$2-3	$5-6	$9-12
824-150-1/2/4, 1985	$2-3	$5-6	$9-12
Inserts			
Sticker	$5-6	$10-13	$20-25
Merchandise sheet	$1-2	$3-4	$5-8
Argentina SUP-772, 1977	$4-5	$8-10	$15-20
Argentina 6154, 1980	$13-15	$25-30	$50-60
Reel-to-reel tape			
1 R1 6589 (USA, 1976)	$9-13	$18-25	$35-50
Love Gun			
LPs, NBLP-7057 (1977)			
Filmworks label	$5-6	$10-13	$20-25
Promotional	$9-10	$18-20	$35-40
Test pressing	$20-25	$40-50	$80-100
Acetate	$20-25	$40-50	$80-100
The Originals II			
LPs, Japan			
VIP-5504-6 (complete)	$75-81	$150-163	$300-325

Rock and Roll Over, Argentina, 1980.

Rock and Roll Over, reel-to-reel tape.

The Originals II, Japan.

Item	VG	EX	NM
Inserts			
Lyric booklet	$4-5	$8-10	$15-20
Photo booklet	$4-5	$8-10	$15-20
Masks, each	$3-4	$6-8	$12-15
OBI strip	$3-4	$6-8	$12-15
Alive II			
LPs, USA, NBLP-7076 (1977)			
Filmworks label	$4-5	$8-10	$15-20
Promotional	$19-20	$38-40	$75-80
Test pressing	$50-56	$100-113	$200-225
Acetate	$20-25	$40-50	$80-100
Error copy lists 3 extra songs	$88-100	$175-200	$350-400
822-781-1 (1985)	$3-4	$6-8	$12-15
Inserts			
Booklet	$3-4	$6-8	$12-15
Tattoos	$2-3	$5-6	$9-12
Merchandise sheet	$1-2	$3-4	$5-8
Argentina SUP-984, 1977	$20-25	$40-50	$80-100
Argentina SUP-985, 1977	$20-25	$40-50	$80-100
France CBLA-72005/6, 1977	$5-6	$10-13	$20-25
Germany NB-7027, 1977	$5-6	$10-13	$20-25
UK CALD-5004			
Black vinyl, 1977	$5-6	$10-13	$20-25
Red vinyl, 1977	$19-25	$38-50	$75-100

Alive II, Part One, Argentina.

Alive II, Part Two, Argentina.

Alive II, red vinyl, England.

Item	VG	EX	NM
Greatest Hits			
LPs, Korea Dove 53, 1977	$50-56	$100-113	$200-225
Double Platinum			
LPs, USA, NBLP-7100 (1978)			
Filmworks label	$4-5	$8-10	$15-20
Promotional	$16-19	$33-38	$65-75
Test pressing	$50-56	$100-113	$200-225
Acetate	$20-25	$40-50	$80-100
824-155-1 (1985)	$4-5	$8-10	$15-20
The Guitar Technique of Ace Frehley/KISS			
LPs, Japan YX-6126, 1978	$38-44	$75-88	$150-175
Lo Mejor De KISS			
LPs, Argentina, SUP 2408-800199, 1978	$25-31	$50-63	$100-125
Gene Simmons			
LPs, USA, NBLP-7120 (1978)			
Filmworks label	$2-3	$5-6	$9-12
Promotional	$6-8	$13-15	$25-30
Test pressing	$20-25	$40-50	$80-100
Acetate	$20-25	$40-50	$80-100
826-239-1 (1985)	$2-3	$5-6	$9-12

Guitar Technique of Ace Frehley, KISS, Japan.

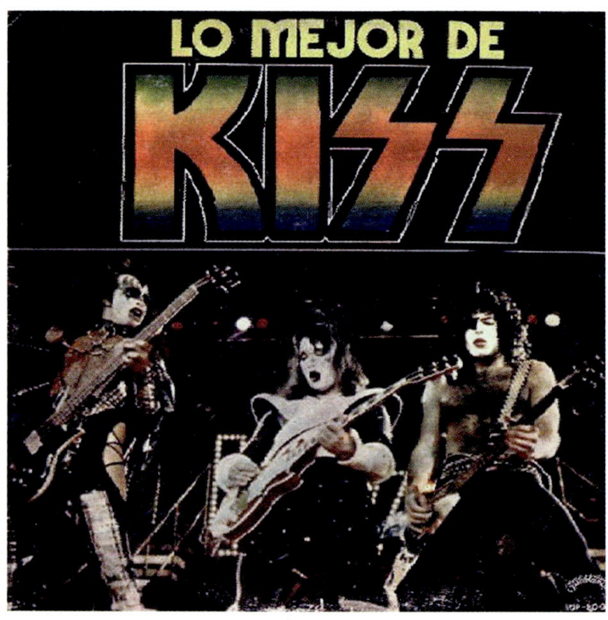

Lo Mejor de KISS, Argentina.

Item	VG	EX	NM
Ace Frehley			
LPs, USA, NBLP-7121 (1978)			
Filmworks label	$2-3	$5-6	$9-12
Promotional	$6-8	$13-15	$25-30
Test pressing	$20-25	$40-50	$80-100
Acetate	$20-25	$40-50	$80-100
826-916-1 (1985)	$2-3	$5-6	$9-12
Peter Criss			
LPs, USA, NBLP-7122 (1978)			
Filmworks label	$2-3	$5-6	$9-12
Promotional	$6-8	$13-15	$25-30
Test pressing	$20-25	$40-50	$80-100
Acetate	$20-25	$40-50	$80-100
826-917-1 (1985)	$2-3	$5-6	$9-12
Paul Stanley			
LPs, USA, NBLP-7123 (1978)			
Filmworks label	$2-3	$5-6	$9-12
Promotional	$6-8	$13-15	$25-30
Test pressing	$20-25	$40-50	$80-100
Acetate	$20-25	$40-50	$80-100
826-915-1 (1985)	$2-3	$5-6	$9-12
Solo album box set,			
Japan VIP-6577-6580, 1979	$100-113	$200-225	$400-450

Item	VG	EX	NM
Best of Solo Albums			
Argentina 6399-075, 1980	$8-10	$15-20	$30-40
Australia NBL P2, 1979	$4-5	$8-10	$15-20
France CB-71057, 1979	$8-10	$15-20	$30-40
Germany NB-7060, 1979	$3-4	$6-8	$12-15
Germany 6302-060, 1980	$3-4	$6-8	$12-15
Mexico 6302-060, 1980	$8-10	$15-20	$30-40
Dynasty			
LPs			
USA, NBLP-7152 (1979)			
Filmworks label	$4-5	$8-10	$15-20
Promotional	$13-15	$25-30	$50-60
Test pressing	$20-25	$40-50	$80-100
Acetate	$20-25	$40-50	$80-100
812-770-1 (1985)	$2-3	$5-6	$9-12
Germany			
NB-7049, red vinyl, 1979	$15-19	$30-38	$60-75
NB-7049, 1979	$4-5	$8-10	$15-20
9128-024	$4-5	$8-10	$15-20
Japan			
VIP-6678 red obi, 1979	$11-13	$23-25	$45-50
22S-11 yellow obi, 1980	$8-9	$15-18	$30-35
R00C-2021 crazy obi, 1984	$5-8	$10-15	$20-30
PHJR-20012 white vinyl from box set, 1998	$11-13	$23-25	$45-50

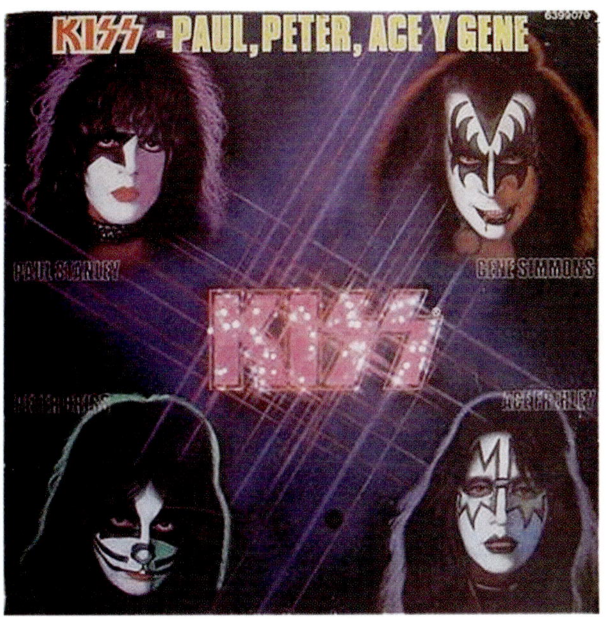

KISS-Paul, Peter, Ace and Gene, Argentina.

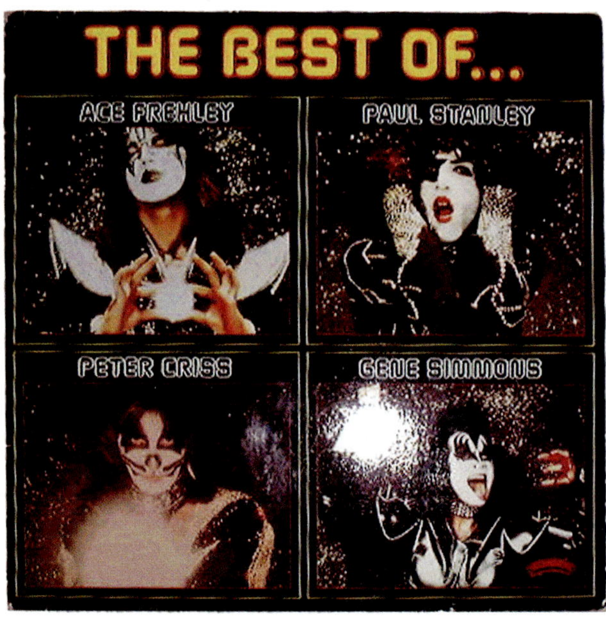

The Best of Ace Frehley, Paul Stanley, Peter Criss, Gene Simmons, France. Rick Reese collection.

KISS, Best of Solo Albums, Germany, NB-7060.

Dynasty, reel-to-reel tape. Jeff Barre Collection.

Item	VG	EX	NM
Mexico LPR-43032, 1979	$4-5	$8-10	$15-20
South Africa NAL-7060	$4-5	$8-10	$15-20
UK CALH-2051, 1979	$4-5	$8-10	$15-20
Reel-to-Reel tape			
1R1 6994 (USA, 1979)	$20-25	$40-50	$80-100
Unmasked			
LPs			
USA, NBLP-7225 (1980)			
Filmworks label	$4-5	$8-10	$15-20
Promotional	$13-15	$25-30	$50-60

Item	VG	EX	NM
Test pressing	$20-25	$40-50	$80-100
Acetate	$20-25	$40-50	$80-100
800-041-1 (1985)	$2-3	$5-6	$9-12
Australia 6302-032, 1980	$4-5	$8-10	$15-20
Germany 6302-032, 1980	$4-5	$8-10	$15-20
Japan			
25S-3 yellow obi, 1980	$8-9	$15-18	$30-35
R00C-2022 crazy obi, 1984	$5-8	$10-15	$20-30
Mexico LPR-43038 (1980)			
Black vinyl	$4-5	$8-10	$15-20
Multi color swirl vinyl	$13-15	$25-30	$50-60
Translucent yellow swirl vinyl	$15-19	$30-38	$60-75
Gold vinyl (might be yellow)	$15-19	$30-38	$60-75
Yellow vinyl	$15-19	$30-38	$60-75
Clear vinyl (rumored to exist)	$15-19	$30-38	$60-75
South Africa STAR-5217	$4-5	$8-10	$15-20
UK 6302-032, 1980	$4-5	$8-10	$15-20
Music from "The Elder"			
LPs, USA, NBLP-7261 (1981)			
Hand label	$9-11	$18-23	$35-45
Promotional	$31-38	$63-75	$125-150
Test pressing	$20-25	$40-50	$80-100
Acetate	$20-25	$40-50	$80-100
824 153-1 (1985)	$2-3	$5-6	$9-12
Turkey	$38-50	$75-100	$150-200

Unmasked, swirl vinyl, Mexico.

Music From the Elder, Turkey.

Item	VG	EX	NM
Killers			
LPs			
Test pressing	$20-25	$40-50	$80-100
Acetate	$20-25	$40-50	$80-100
Australia 6302-193, 1982	$4-5	$8-10	$15-20
Germany 6302-193, 1982	$4-5	$8-10	$15-20
Germany 812-771-1, 1982	$4-5	$8-10	$15-20
Creatures of the Night			
Makeup cover			
LPs, USA, NBLP-7270 (1982)			
Black logo label	$5-6	$10-13	$20-25
Promotional	$9-11	$18-23	$35-45
Test pressing	$20-25	$40-50	$80-100
Acetate	$20-25	$40-50	$80-100
Filmworks label (1983)	$6-8	$13-15	$25-30
824-154-1 (1985)	$3-4	$6-8	$12-15
Hotter Than Metal			
LPs, Holland HRS-23, 1982	$4-5	$8-10	$15-20
Superstar			
LPs, Italy SU-0123, 1982	$4-5	$8-10	$15-20
The KISS Collection: box set			
LPs, Brazil 814-211-1, 1983	$50-56	$100-113	$200-225

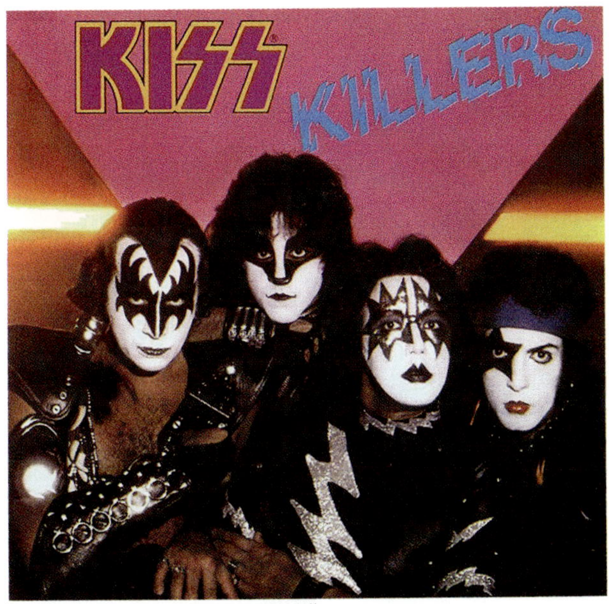

KISS Killers.

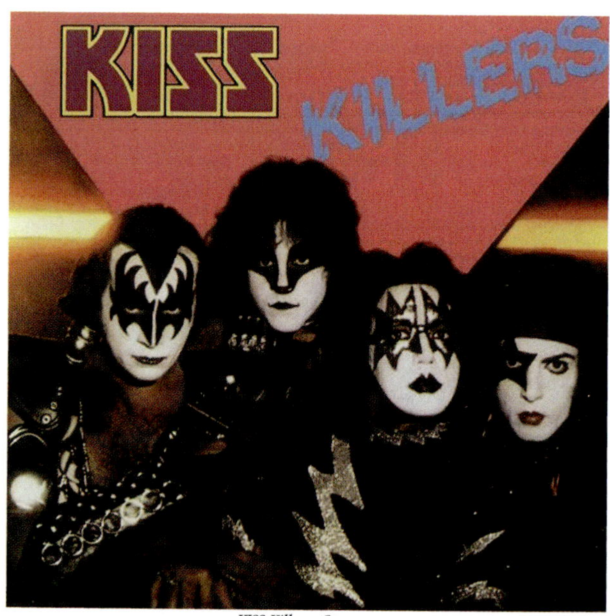

KISS Killers, Germany.

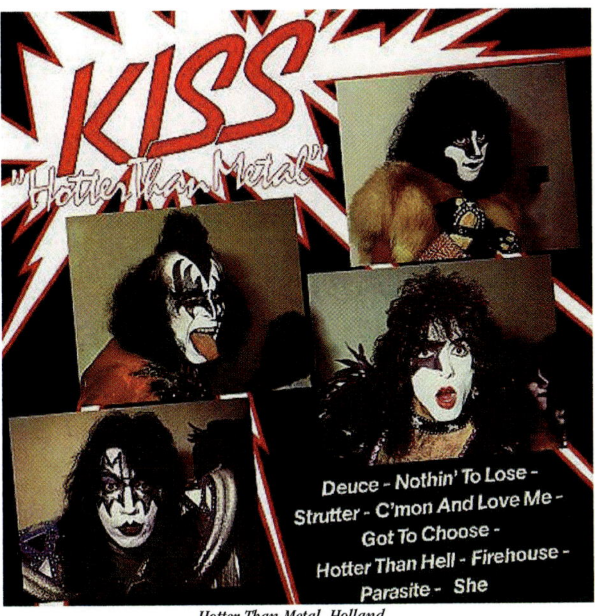

Hotter Than Metal, Holland.

Superstar, Italy. Sean Reid collection.

Item	VG	EX	NM
Lick it Up			
LPs, USA, 814-297-1 (1983)			
Mercury label	$2-3	$5-6	$9-12
Promotional	$4-5	$8-10	$15-20
Test pressing	$10-13	$20-25	$40-50
Acetate	$10-13	$20-25	$40-50
Germany VERL-9, 1983	$4-5	$8-10	$15-20
Holland VERL-9, 1983	$4-5	$8-10	$15-20
Japan			
28S-181 false front obi, 1983	$10-13	$20-25	$40-50
R00C-2026 crazy obi, 1984	$6-8	$13-15	$25-30
CDs, USA			
814-297-2, 1983	$1-2	$3-4	$5-8
558-859-2, 1998	$1-2	$3-4	$5-8
30 Anõs De Musica Rock			
LPs, Mexico 822-305-1, 1984	$13-15	$25-30	$50-60
Con Todo El Poder De La Musica			
LPs, Mexico 822-305-1, 1984	$13-15	$25-30	$50-60

The KISS Collection box set, Brazil. Rick Reese collection.

Lick It Up, Japan, 1983.

Lick It Up CD, long sheet.

30 Anos De Musica Rock, Mexico.

Con Todo El Poder De La Musica, Mexico.

Item	VG	EX	NM
Animalize			
LPs, USA, 822-495-1 (1984)			
Mercury label	$2-3	$5-6	$9-12
Promotional	$4-5	$8-10	$15-20
Test pressing	$10-13	$20-25	$40-50
Acetate	$10-13	$20-25	$40-50
O' Rock De KISS			
Brazil 818-981-0, 1985	$19-25	$38-50	$75-100
Rockanroleando Toda La Noche			
Mexico LPR-43073, 1985	$10-13	$20-25	$40-50
Asylum			
LPs, USA, 826-099-1 (1985)			
Mercury label	$2-3	$5-6	$9-12
Promotional	$4-5	$8-10	$15-20
Test pressing	$10-13	$20-25	$40-50
Acetate	$10-13	$20-25	$40-50
KISS The Singles			
LPs, Australia CC0013-C, 1985	$19-25	$38-50	$75-100
Cassettes, Australia MX2-10270, 1985	$4-5	$8-10	$15-20

O Rock De KISS, Brazil.

Rockanroleando Toda La Noche, Mexico.

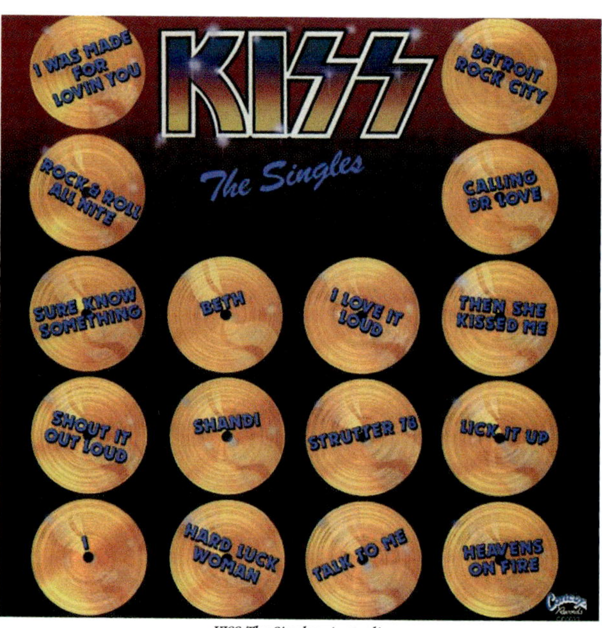

KISS The Singles, Australia.

Item	VG	EX	NM
Crazy Nights			
LPs, USA, 832-626-1 (1987)			
Mercury label	$2-3	$5-6	$9-12
Promotional	$4-5	$8-10	$15-20
Test pressing	$10-13	$20-25	$40-50
Acetate	$10-13	$20-25	$40-50
Chikara			
CDs (many counterfeits exist)			
Japan P30R-20008, 1988	$31-38	$63-75	$125-150
Picture discs, bootleg, never released in any format except CD	$2-3	$5-6	$9-12
Smashes, Thrashes and Hits			
LPs, USA, 836-427-1 (1988)			
Mercury label	$2-3	$5-6	$9-12
Promotional	$4-5	$8-10	$15-20
Test pressing	$10-13	$20-25	$40-50
Acetate	$10-13	$20-25	$40-50
Smashes, Thrashes and Hits: 15 Years of KISStory			
Picture discs, USA 836-887-1, 1989	$10-13	$20-25	$40-50

Chikara, Japan.

Item	VG	EX	NM
Hot in the Shade			
LPs, USA, 838-913-1 (1989)			
Mercury label	$4-5	$8-10	$15-20
Promotional	$8-9	$15-18	$30-35
Test pressing	$13-15	$25-30	$50-60
Acetate	$13-15	$25-30	$50-60
Revenge			
LPs, USA, 848-037-1 (1993, released one year after the CD)			
Mercury label			
Blue vinyl	$3-4	$6-8	$12-15
Gray vinyl	$3-4	$6-8	$12-15
Promotional Does Not Exist	$0-0	$0-0	$0-0
Test pressing	$10-13	$20-25	$40-50
Acetate	$10-13	$20-25	$40-50
Cassettes, USA			
848-037-4, 1992	$0-1	$1-2	$1-3
Promotional advance release	$2-3	$5-6	$9-12
Alive III			
LPs, USA, 522-647-1 (1994)			
Red vinyl	$5-6	$10-13	$20-25
White vinyl	$5-6	$10-13	$20-25
Blue vinyl	$5-6	$10-13	$20-25
Black vinyl	$6-8	$13-15	$25-30
Promotional	$6-8	$13-15	$25-30

Revenge, advance release cassette. Jeff Barre collection.

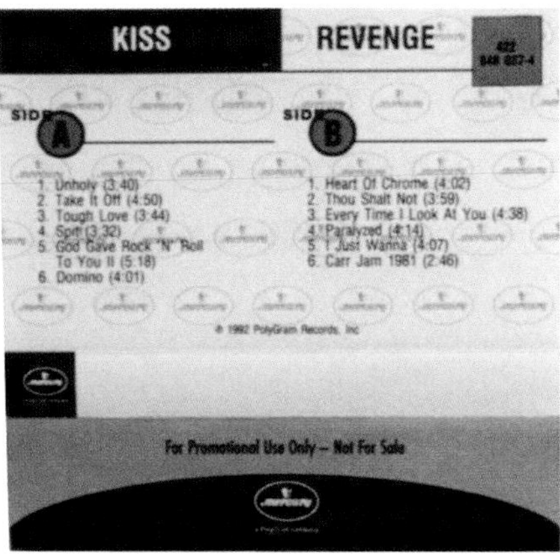

Item	VG	EX	NM
Test pressing	$10-13	$20-25	$40-50
Acetate	$10-13	$20-25	$40-50
CDs			
USA			
514-777-2, 1993	$1-2	$3-4	$5-8
Promotional advance release	$5-6	$10-13	$20-25
Europe and Australia 514-827-2, 1993	$1-2	$3-4	$5-8
Australia Reissue w/bonus EP, 1995	$4-5	$8-10	$15-20
Japan PHCR-1198, 1993	$4-5	$8-10	$15-20
Cassettes			
USA			
514-777-4, 1993	$0-1	$1-2	$1-3
Promotional advance release	$2-3	$5-6	$9-12
Europe 514-827-4, 1993	$0-1	$1-2	$1-3
MTV Unplugged			
USA, 528-950-1 (1996)			
Mercury label			
Black vinyl	$4-5	$8-10	$15-20
Yellow vinyl	$5-6	$10-13	$20-25
You Wanted the Best...You've Got the Best!			
LPs, USA, 532-741-1 (1996)			
Logo label	$5-6	$10-13	$20-25
Promotional	$11-13	$23-25	$45-50
Test pressing	$13-15	$25-30	$50-60
Acetate	$13-15	$25-30	$50-60

Alive III, advance release cassette. Jeff Barre collection.

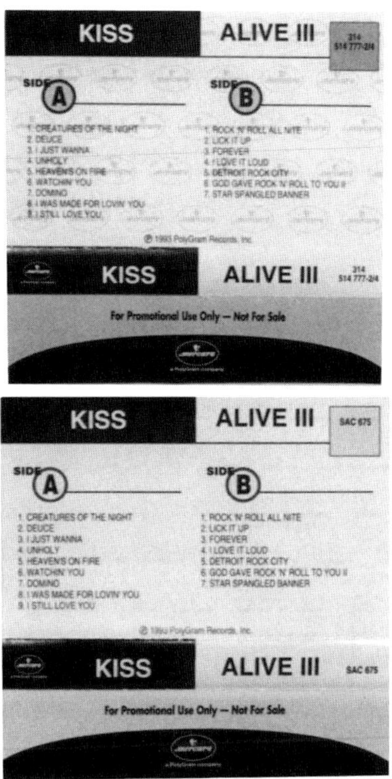

Alive III, with bonus EP disc, Australia.

Item	VG	EX	NM
Cassettes			
USA			
532-741-4, 1996	$0-1	$1-2	$1-3
Promotional advance release	$2-3	$5-6	$9-12
Europe 532-741-4, 1996	$0-1	$1-2	$1-3
Greatest KISS			
(No known LP release)			
CDs, USA			
534-725-2, 1997	$1-2	$3-4	$5-8
Promotional advance release	$5-6	$10-13	$20-25

Greatest KISS, Australia.

Greatest KISS, England.

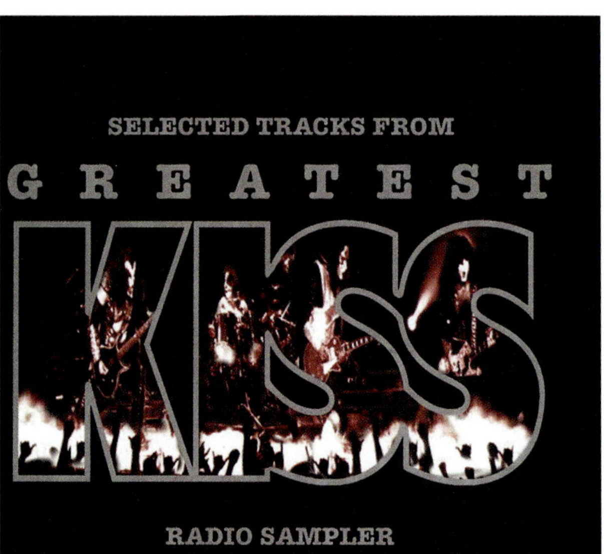

Greatest KISS radio sampler, UK and German promo 578-889-2, 1976.

Item	VG	EX	NM
Australia 534-299-2, silver slip	$8-10	$15-20	$30-40
Case, gold CD, 1996			
Europe 534-299-2, 1996	$1-2	$3-4	$5-8
UK and German promo, 578-889-2, 1996	$8-10	$15-20	$30-40
Japan PHRC-1500, 1996	$4-5	$8-10	$15-20
Japan PHRC-94012, 1998	$4-5	$8-10	$15-20
Greatest Hits			
CDs, UK TV 536-159-2, 1997	$2-3	$5-6	$9-12
Cassettes, UK TV 536-159-4, 1997	$1-1	$2-3	$3-5
Carnival of Souls: The Final Sessions			
LPs, no American LP release			
Color vinyl LPs			
Counterfeit, never officially released	$5-6	$10-13	$20-25
Picture discs			
Counterfeit, never officially released	$5-6	$10-13	$20-25
CDs			
USA			
536-323-2, 1997	$1-2	$3-4	$5-8
Promotional advance release	$5-6	$10-13	$20-25
Europe, 536-323-2, 1997	$1-2	$3-4	$5-8
Japan, PHRC-1560, 1997	$4-5	$8-10	$15-20

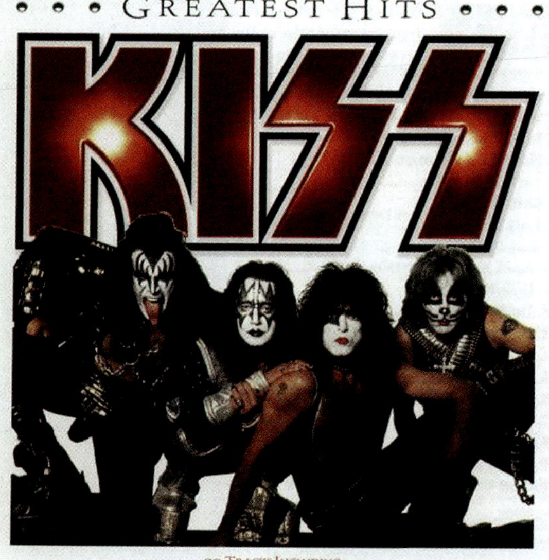

Greatest Hits CD, England.

Item	VG	EX	NM
The Originals 1974-1978			
CDs, Japan promo box set of 10	$25-31	$50-63	$100-125
Retail releases Digipak CDs, box only.			
The Originals 1974-1979			
Japan only			
Promo box to store retail release CDs	$25-31	$50-63	$100-125
Digipack CDs, single disc	$6-8	$13-15	$25-30
Digipack CDs, double disc	$13-19	$25-38	$50-75
Psycho Circus			
LPs (no American LP release)			
Picture discs (counterfeit, never officially released)	$5-6	$10-13	$20-25
CDs, USA (1998)			
MEAD-169, promo	$8-9	$15-18	$30-35
Cassettes, USA			
558-992-4, 1998	$1-2	$3-4	$5-8
Promotional advance release	$2-3	$5-6	$9-12
Europe 558-992-4, 1998	$1-2	$3-4	$5-8

The Originals 1974-1979, LP box set, black, Japan.

Psycho Circus advance promotional release CD.

Digi Pack CDs, Japan.

Psycho Circus advance release cassette.

Psycho Circus, plus live EP, Europe.

Item	VG	EX	NM
Psycho Circus + Live EP			
CDs, Europe 538 938-2, 1999	$4-5	$8-10	$15-20
The Box Set			
CDs, USA, 586 561-2 (2001)			
Standard box	$11-15	$23-30	$45-60
Mini guitar case box	$25-31	$50-63	$100-125
Gold edition box	$150-188	$300-375	$600-750

Item	VG	EX	NM
Japan, 2001			
UICY-7088/92, standard box	$11-15	$23-30	$45-60
UICY-7093/97 mini guitar case	$25-31	$50-63	$100-125
UK, 2001			
586 561-2, standard box	$11-15	$23-30	$45-60
586 555-2 mini guitar case box	$25-31	$50-63	$100-125
KISS: The Very Best of			
CDs, USA			
440 063 122-2 (2002)	$1-2	$3-4	$5-7
The Best of KISS			
CDs, USA			
B0000827-02 (2003)	$1-2	$3-4	$5-7
The Best of KISS Volume 2			
CDs, USA			
B002549-02 (2003)	$1-2	$3-4	$5-7
KISS Gold			
CDs and DVD, USA			
B0003419-00 (2004)	$9-10	$18-20	$35-40
CDs, USA			
B0003077-02	$4-5	$8-10	$15-20

Item	VG	EX	NM

45 singles and extended plays (EPs)

All entries are from the USA, unless noted; long B-side titles are abbreviated. All non-USA entries are assumed to have been issued with picture sleeve or insert, unless noted.

(More than 280 worldwide KISS picture sleeves can be seen at www.kisshall.com)

Item	VG	EX	NM
Nothin' To Lose/Love Theme From KISS			
USA NEB 004			
Casablanca blue label	$4-5	$8-9	$15-18
Promo mono / stereo	$5-6	$10-13	$20-25
Australia NEB 0004 (color vinyl)	$4-5	$8-10	$15-20
UK CBX-503 no picture sleeve	$9-13	$18-25	$35-50
Nothin' To Lose/Kissin' Time/Strutter/Deuce			
Brazil CBCD - 771	$20-25	$40-50	$80-100
Kissin' Time/Nothin To Lose			
USA NEB 0011			
Casablanca blue label	$8-9	$15-18	$30-35
Promo mono/stereo	$5-6	$10-13	$20-25
Strutter/100,000 Years			
USA NEB 0015			
Casablanca blue label	$13-15	$25-30	$50-60
100,000 years often written as 100,00 on many copies			
Promo mono stereo	$9-10	$18-20	$35-40

Item	VG	EX	NM
Let Me Go, Rock and Roll/Hotter Than Hell			
USA NB 823			
Casablanca blue label	$50-56	$100-113	$200-225
Promo mono/stereo	$19-25	$38-50	$75-100
Filmworks label	$4-5	$8-9	$15-18
Germany BF 18501	$13-19	$25-38	$50-75
Rock and Roll All Nite/Getaway			
USA NB 829			
Casablanca blue label	$4-5	$8-9	$15-18
Promo mono/stereo	$5-6	$10-13	$20-25
Germany C006 96694	$13-19	$25-38	$50-75
Holland NG 829	$25-31	$50-63	$100-125
Italy	$31-38	$63-75	$125-150
C'mon And Love Me/Getaway			
USA NB 841			
Casablanca blue label	$5-6	$10-13	$20-25
Promo mono stereo	$5-6	$10-13	$20-25
Filmworks label	$3-4	$6-8	$12-15
Germany BF 18502	$13-19	$25-38	$50-75
Japan Jet 2335	$11-13	$23-25	$45-50
Rock and Roll All Nite - Live/Studio			
USA NB 850			
Casablanca blue label	$2-2	$3-5	$6-9
Promo mono/stereo	$4-5	$8-9	$15-18

Nothin' to Lose, Casablanca label.

Nothin' to Lose, Australia. Lloyd Kellett collection.

KISS EP, Nothin' to Lose, Brazil. Julian Gill collection.

Let Me Go Rock and Roll, promotional blue label.

Rock and Roll All Nite, Germany. Julian Gill collection.

Item	VG	EX	NM
Promo stereo/stereo	$10-13	$20-25	$40-50
Filmworks label	$3-4	$6-8	$12-15
Germany BF 18505	$9-10	$18-20	$35-40
Holland NG 829	$63-65	$125-130	$250-260
Rock and Roll All Nite/Two Timer/C'mon and Love Me/Anything for My Baby			
Brazil CBCD - 794	$19-25	$38-50	$75-100
Shout It Out Loud/Sweet Pain			
USA NB 854			
Casablanca blue label	$2-2	$3-5	$6-9
Promo mono/stereo	$4-5	$8-9	$15-18
Filmworks label	$2-2	$3-5	$6-9
Denmark GBX 516 (may be live)	$19-25	$38-50	75-100
Germany BF 18503	$19-25	$38-50	$75-100
Germany C006 97669	$8-9	$15-18	$30-35
Flaming Youth/God of Thunder			
USA NB 858			
Camel label	$2-2	$3-5	$6-9
Promo mono/stereo	$4-5	$8-9	$15-18
Picture sleeve	$5-6	$10-13	$20-25
Detroit Rock City/Beth			
USA NB 863			
Camel label	$2-3	$5-6	$9-12
Promo mono/stereo	$4-5	$8-9	$15-18

C'Mon and Love Me, blue and Filmworks label variants.

C'Mon and Love Me, Germany. Julian Gill collection.

Rock and Roll All Nite, rare promotional stereo/stereo version.

Dressed to Kill EP, Brazil, CBCD-794. Julian Gill collection.

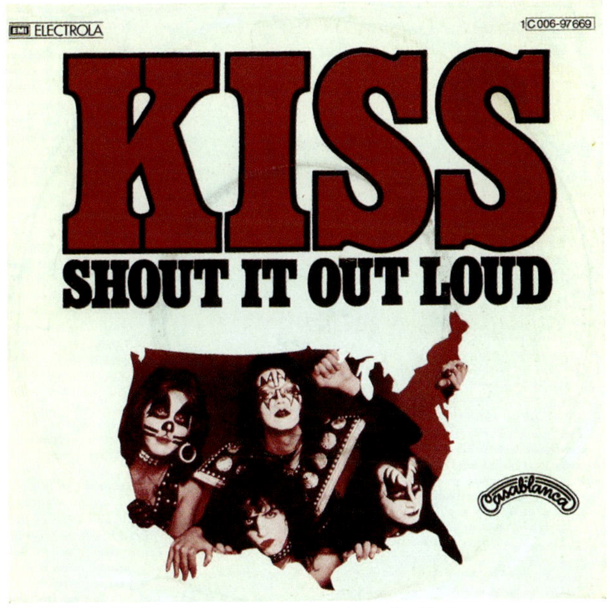

Shout It Out Loud, Germany. Julian Gill collection.

Item	VG	EX	NM
Beth/Detroit Rock City			
USA NB 863			
Camel label	$2-2	$3-5	$6-9
Filmworks label	$1-2	$3-4	$5-8
Beth/Detroit Rock City			
USA NBX-863			
Camel label Promo mono/stereo	$4-5	$8-9	$15-18
Beth/Beth-Mono/Stereo-Beth			
USA 1DJ			
Camel label Promo mono/stereo	$4-5	$8-9	$15-18
Hard Luck Woman/Mr. Speed			
USA NB 873			
Camel label	$1-2	$3-4	$5-8
Promo mono/stereo	$4-5	$8-9	$15-18
Hard Luck Woman/Calling Dr. Love/Beth			
UK CAN 102	$5-6	$10-13	$20-25
Calling Dr. Love/Take Me			
USA NB 880			
Camel label	$2-2	$3-5	$6-9
Promo mono/stereo	$4-5	$8-9	$15-18
Filmworks label	$1-2	$3-4	$5-8

Hard Luck Woman, England. Lloyd Kellett collection.

Christine 16/Shock Me, France. Lloyd Kellett collection.

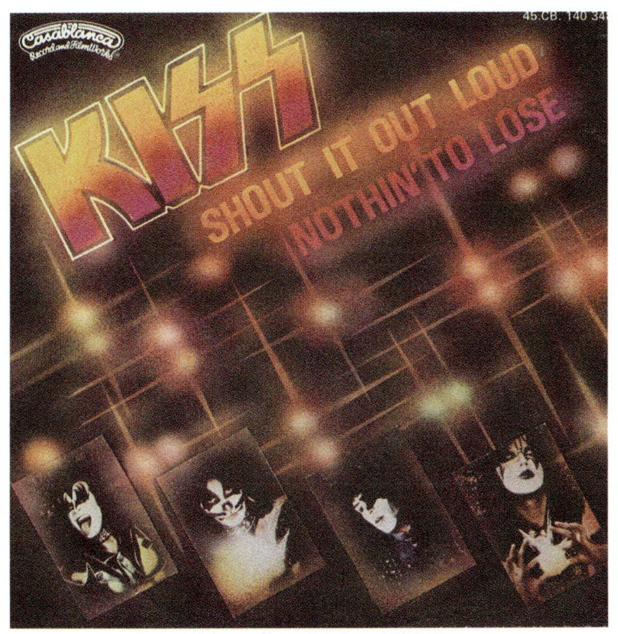

Shout It Out Loud, France. Julian Gill Collection.

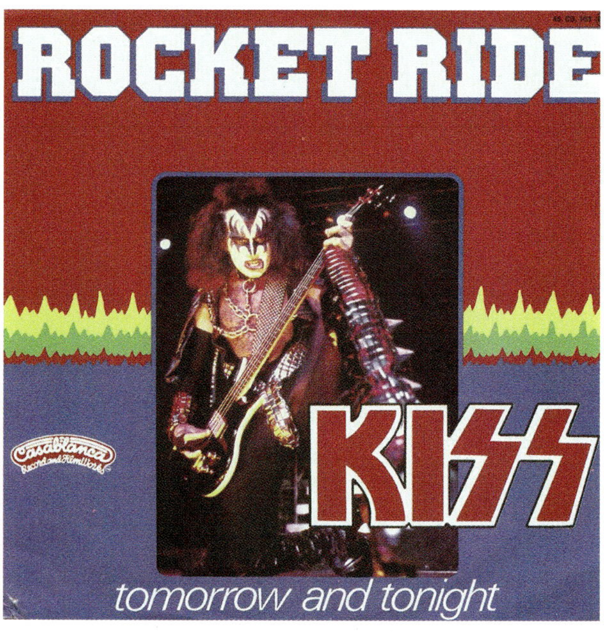

Rocket Ride, France. Julian Gill Collection.

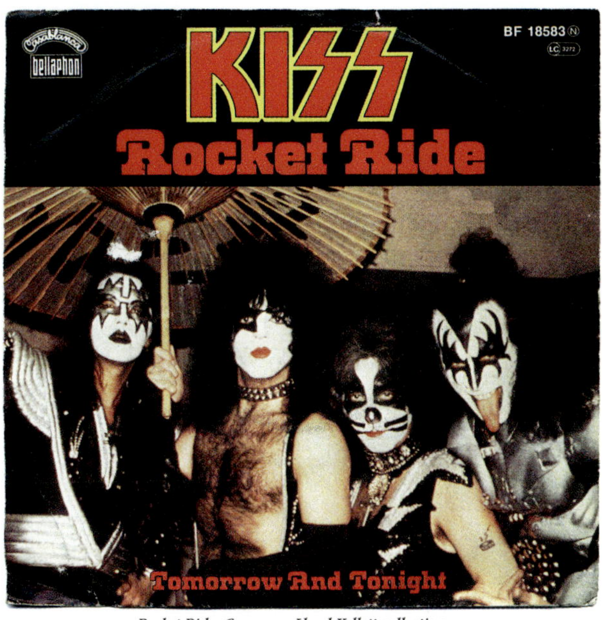

Rocket Ride, Germany. Lloyd Kellett collection.

Item	VG	EX	NM
France CB 140 226	$8-9	$15-18	$30-35
Germany BF 18520	$8-9	$15-18	$30-35
Japan VIP 2525	$8-9	$15-18	$30-35
Christine Sixteen/Shock Me (2:52 version)			
USA NB 889			
Camel label	$1-2	$3-4	$5-8
Filmworks label	$1-2	$3-4	$5-8
Filmworks promo label, NB 889DJ	$4-5	$8-9	$15-18
France CB 140290	$8-9	$15-18	$30-35
Love Gun/Hooligan			
USA NB 895			
Filmworks label	$1-2	$3-4	$5-8
Filmworks promo label NB 895DJ	$4-5	$8-9	$15-18
Shout It Out Loud (live)/Nothin' To Lose			
USA NB 906			
Filmworks label	$1-2	$3-4	$5-8
Filmworks promo label, NB 906DJ	$4-5	$8-9	$15-18
Denmark GBX 516	$8-9	$15-18	$30-35
France CB 140348	$8-9	$15-18	$30-35
Germany BF 18571	$8-9	$15-18	$30-35
Italy CA 508	$8-9	$15-18	$30-35
Japan VIP 2584	$8-9	$15-18	$30-35

Strutter 78, Mexico. EP Lloyd Kellett collection.

Rare Strutter '78 Camel label variant.

Strutter '78, France. Lloyd Kellett collection.

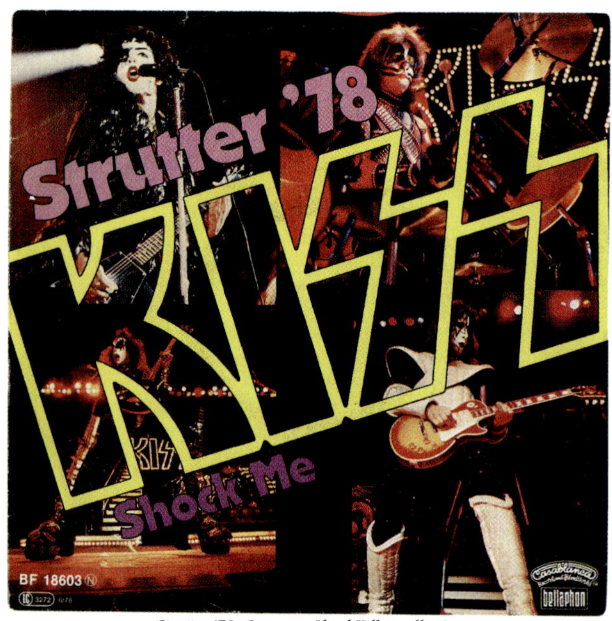

Strutter '78, Germany. Lloyd Kellett collection.

Item	VG	EX	NM
Rocket Ride/Tomorrow and Tonight			
USA NB 915			
Filmworks label	$1-2	$3-4	$5-8
Filmworks promo label NB 915DJ	$4-5	$8-9	$15-18
France CB 103	$8-9	$15-18	$30-35
Germany BF 18583	$8-9	$15-18	$30-35
Japan VIP 2603	$8-9	$15-18	$30-35
Sweden 7C 005-60583	$20-25	$40-50	$80-100
Strutter '78/Let Me Go, Rock and Roll/Love Gun/Beth			
Mexico 2453	$8-9	$15-18	$30-35
Strutter '78/Shock Me			
USA NB 928			
Camel label	$8-9	$15-18	$30-35
Filmworks label	$1-2	$3-4	$5-8
Filmworks promo label NB 928DJ	$4-5	$8-9	$15-18
France CB 157	$8-9	$15-18	$30-35
Germany BF 18603	$8-9	$15-18	$30-35
Japan VIP 2638	$8-9	$15-18	$30-35
Radioactive/Hold Me Touch Me/New York Groove/Don't You Let Me Down			
Mexico 2463	$8-9	$15-18	$30-35

Solos EP, Mexico 2463. Lloyd Kellett collection.

Rare 1978 Ace Frehley New York Groove Camel label variant.

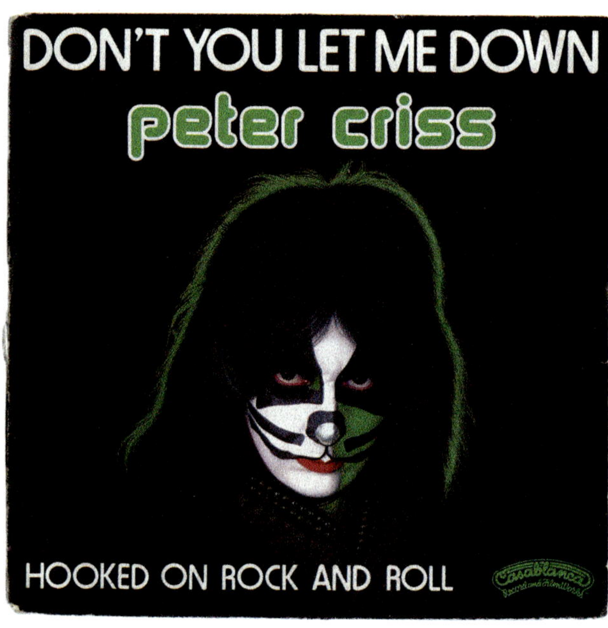

Peter Solo, France. Lloyd Kellett collection.

I Was Made For Lovin' You, pink vinyl, Germany. Julian Gill collection.

Item	VG	EX	NM
Hold Me, Touch Me/Goodbye			
USA NB 940			
Filmworks label	$1-2	$3-4	$5-8
Filmworks promo label NB 940DJ	$4-5	$8-9	$15-18
Casablanca Camel label	$3-4	$6-8	$12-15
New York Groove/Snow Blind			
USA NB 941			
Filmworks label	$1-2	$3-4	$5-8
Filmworks promo label NB 941DJ	$4-5	$8-9	$15-18
Casablanca Camel label	$3-4	$6-8	$12-15
Radioactive/See You In Your Dreams			
USA NB951			
Filmworks label	$1-2	$3-4	$5-8
Filmworks promo label NB 951DJ	$4-5	$8-9	$15-18
Don't You Let Me Down/Hooked on Rock and Roll			
USA NB952			
Filmworks label	$1-2	$3-4	$5-8
Filmworks promo label NB 952DJ	$4-5	$8-9	$15-18
France CB 1130	$6-8	$13-15	$25-30
Germany BF 18643	$6-8	$13-15	$25-30
Italy CA 521	$6-8	$13-15	$25-30
Japan VIP 2692	$9-10	$18-20	$35-40

Sure Know Something, Italy. Lloyd Kellett collection.

Dirty Livin', 12-inch, Germany.

Item	VG	EX	NM
You Still Matter To Me/Hooked on Rock and Roll			
USA NB 961			
Filmworks label	$1-2	$3-4	$5-8
Filmworks promo label NB 961DJ	$4-5	$8-9	$15-18
UK CAN 139			
Green vinyl, mask	$18-19	$35-38	$70-75
Black vinyl	$6-8	$13-15	$25-30
I Was Made For Lovin' You/Hard Times			
USA NB 983			
Filmworks label	$1-2	$2-3	$3-6
Filmworks promo label NB 983DJ	$3-4	$6-8	$12-15
Belgium	$15-20	$30-40	$60-80
France			
CB 1182	$4-5	$8-9	$15-18
CB 1182 (disco rock)	$4-5	$8-9	$15-18
Germany BF 18667			
Black vinyl	$4-5	$8-9	$15-18
Red vinyl	$13-16	$25-33	$50-65
Pink vinyl	$13-16	$25-33	$50-65
6175 014, censored logo	$4-5	$8-9	$15-18
Sure Know Something/Dirty Livin'			
USA NB2205			
Filmworks label	$1-2	$3-4	$5-8
Filmworks promo NB NB2205DJ	$4-5	$8-9	$15-18

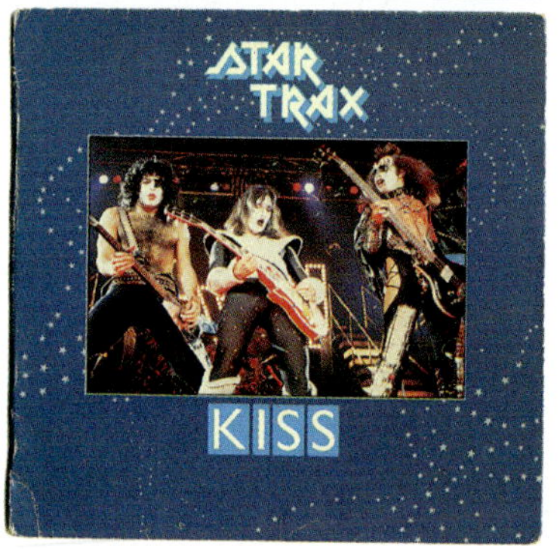

Star Trax, Australia, both variations. Lloyd Kellett collection.

2000 Man, England. Lloyd Kellett collection.

Shandi, France. Lloyd Kellett collection.

Shandi, Italy. Lloyd Kellett collection.

Item	VG	EX	NM
Germany BF 18684	$8-9	$15-18	$30-35
Italy CA 528	$8-9	$15-18	$30-35
Japan VIP 2775	$8-9	$15-18	$30-35
Spain 6175-023	$8-9	$15-18	$30-35
UK CAN-163, no picture sleeve	$3-4	$6-8	$12-15
Dirty Livin'/Sure Know Something			
France CB 1226	$4-5	$8-9	$15-18
Germany BF 18684, (double hit)	$8-9	$15-18	$30-35
Star Trax: Rock and Roll All Nite/Shout It Out Loud/Love Gun/Sure Know Something			
Australia			
6200 027, KISS logo	$6-8	$13-15	$25-30
6200 027, generic KISS letters	$6-8	$13-15	$25-30
2000 MAN/I Was Made For Lovin' You/Sure Know			
UK NB 1001	$6-8	$13-15	$25-30
Shandi/She's So European			
USA NB2282			
Filmworks label	$1-2	$3-4	$5-8
Filmworks promo NB NB2282DJ	$4-5	$8-9	$15-18
Belgium NB 2282	$11-14	$23-28	$45-55
France C6000 436	$11-14	$23-28	$45-55

Shandi EP, Mexico. Lloyd Kellett collection.

Magic Touch, France. Lloyd Kellett collection.

Talk To Me, England. Lloyd Kellett collection.

Tomorrow, Austria. Lloyd Kellett collection.

World Without Heroes, picture disc 45, England. Lloyd Kellett collection.

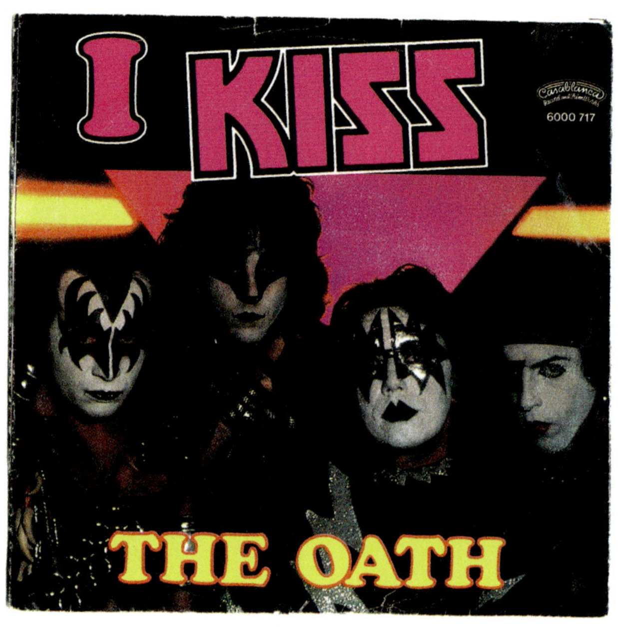

I, Austria. Lloyd Kellett collection.

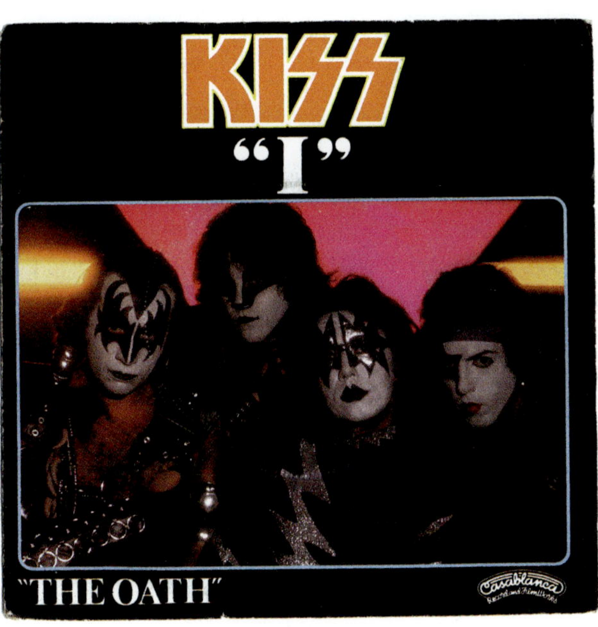

I, France. Lloyd Kellett collection.

I, Holland. Lloyd Kellett collection.

Item	VG	EX	NM
Germany			
6000 436	$11-14	$23-28	$45-55
6000 436 censored logo	$11-14	$23-28	$45-55
Holland 6000 436	$11-14	$23-28	$45-55
Italy CA 539	$8-9	$15-18	$30-35
Japan 6S-6	$8-9	$15-18	$30-35
Mexico 2472	$8-9	$15-18	$30-35
Norway 6000 436	$8-9	$15-18	$30-35
Portugal 6000 436	$8-9	$15-18	$30-35
Spain 6000-436	$8-9	$15-18	$30-35
Sweden 6000 436	$11-14	$23-28	$45-55
Shandi/Mr. Make Believe/Firehouse/Rock and Roll All Nite			
Mexico 2472	$8-9	$15-18	$30-35
Magic Touch/Save Your Love			
France 101259	$8-9	$15-18	$30-35
Talk To Me/She's So European			
UK MER 19	$5-6	$10-13	$20-25
A World Without Heroes/Dark Light			
USA NB2343			
Filmworks label	$1-2	$3-4	$5-8
Filmworks promo NB NB2343DJ	$4-5	$8-9	$15-18

I Love It Loud, Holland. Julian Gill collection.

I Love It Loud, Germany. Lloyd Kellett collection.

Killers, England. Lloyd Kellett collection.

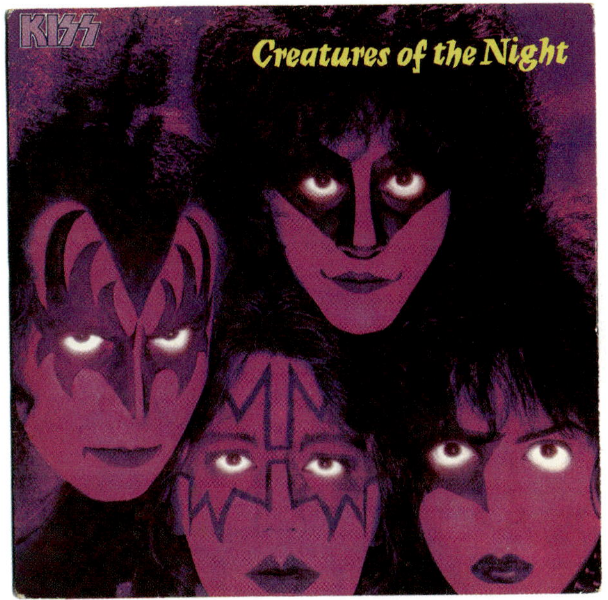

Creatures of the Night, England. Lloyd Kellett collection.

Lick It Up, picture disc 45, England.

Item	VG	EX	NM
Tomorrow/Naked City			
USA NB2299			
Filmworks label	$3-4	$6-8	$12-15
Filmworks promo NB NB2299DJ	$4-5	$8-9	$15-18
Tomorrow/Is That You			
Austria 6000 620, censored logo	$8-9	$15-18	$30-35
Belgium	$8-9	$15-18	$30-35
Germany 6000 620, censored logo	$8-9	$15-18	$30-35
A World Without Heroes/Mr. Blackwell			
UK			
KISS 002	$5-6	$10-13	$20-25
KISS P002, picture disc	$11-13	$23-25	$45-50
I/The Oath			
Australia 6000 717	$8-9	$15-18	$30-35
Austria 6000 717 censored logo	$8-9	$15-18	$30-35
France 6000 717	$8-9	$15-18	$30-35
Italy 6000 717	$8-9	$15-18	$30-35
Germany 6000 717, censored logo	$8-9	$15-18	$30-35
Holland 6000 717	$8-9	$15-18	$30-35
Spain 6000-717	$8-9	$15-18	$30-35
Sweden 6000 717	$8-9	$15-18	$30-35

Lick It Up EP, Mexico. Julian Gill collection.

Uh! All Night, Holland. Lloyd Kellett collection.

Let's Put the X in Sex, Australia. Lloyd Kellett collection.

Hide Your Heart, Australia. Lloyd Kellett collection.

Item	VG	EX	NM
I Love It Loud/Danger			
USA NB 2365			
Filmworks label	$1-2	$3-4	$5-8
Filmworks promo			
NB NB2365DJ	$4-5	$8-9	$15-18
Picture Sleeve	$3-4	$6-8	$12-15
Canada NB 2365	$3-4	$6-8	$12-15
I Love It Loud/Killer			
Germany 6000 911,			
censored logo	$8-9	$15-18	$30-35
Holland 6000 911	$10-13	$20-25	$40-50
Japan 7S-78	$8-9	$15-18	$30-35
Spain 6000-911	$8-9	$15-18	$30-35
Killers/I Love It Loud			
UK KISS 003	$8-9	$15-18	$30-35
Creatures of the Night/Rock and Roll All Nite (Live)			
UK KISS 4	$6-8	$13-15	$25-30
Beth/Hard Luck Woman			
USA 814 303-7			
Time Pieces label	$1-2	$3-4	$5-8
I Was Made For Lovin' You/Rock and Roll All Nite			
USA 814 304-7			
Time Pieces label	$1-2	$3-4	$5-8

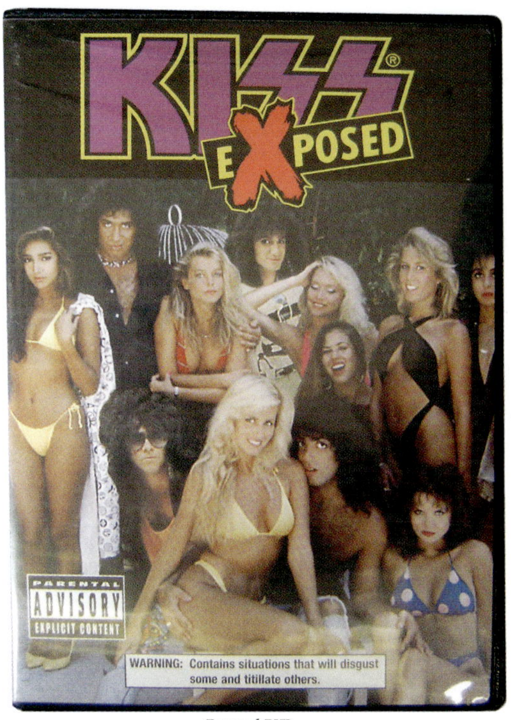
KISS®
EXPOSED
PARENTAL
ADVISORY
EXPLICIT CONTENT
WARNING: Contains situations that will disgust
some and titillate others.

Exposed DVD.

KISS Symphony DVD.

The Best of KISS DVD.

Item	VG	EX	NM
Lick It Up/Dance All Over Your Face			
USA 817 671-7			
Mercury label	$1-1	$2-3	$3-5
Promo, 817 671-7DJ	$2-3	$5-6	$9-12
Lick It Up/Not for the Innocent			
KPIC 5, tank shaped picture disc	$5-6	$10-13	$20-25
Lick It Up/Charisma/I Was Made For Lovin' You/Detroit Rock City			
Mexico	$8-9	$15-18	$30-35
All Hells Breakin' Loose/Young And Wasted			
USA 818 216-7			
Mercury label	$1-1	$2-3	$3-5
Promo label, 818 216-7DJ	$2-3	$5-6	$9-12
Heavens on Fire/Lonely is the Hunter			
USA 880 205-7			
Mercury label	$1-1	$2-3	$3-5
Promo label, 880 205-7DJ	$2-3	$5-6	$9-12
Thrills in the Night/Burn Bitch Burn			
USA 880 535-7			
Mercury label	$1-1	$2-3	$3-5
Promo label, 880 535-7DJ	$2-3	$5-6	$9-12

Item	VG	EX	NM
Tears Are Falling/Any Way You Slice It			
USA 884 141-7			
Mercury label	$1-1	$2-3	$3-5
Promo label, 884 141-7DJ	$2-3	$5-6	$9-12
Picture sleeve	$1-1	$2-3	$3-5
Uh! All Night/Trial By Fire			
Holland 884 487-7	$4-5	$8-9	$15-18
Crazy Crazy Nights/No, No, No			
USA 888 796-7			
Mercury label	$1-1	$2-3	$3-5
Promo label, 888 796-7DJ	$2-3	$5-6	$9-12
Picture sleeve	$1-1	$2-3	$3-5
Reason To Live/Thief in the Night			
USA 870 022-7			
Mercury label	$1-1	$2-3	$3-5
Promo label, 870 022-7DJ	$2-3	$5-6	$9-12
Picture sleeve	$1-1	$2-3	$3-5
Turn on the Night/Hell or High Water			
USA 870 215-7			
Mercury label	$1-1	$2-3	$3-5
Promo label, 870 215-7DJ	$2-3	$5-6	$9-12
Picture sleeve	$1-1	$2-3	$3-5

Item	VG	EX	NM
Let's Put the X In Sex/Calling Dr. Love			
USA 872 246-7			
Mercury label	$1-1	$2-3	$3-5
Promo label, 872 246-7DJ	$2-3	$5-6	$9-12
Picture sleeve	$1-1	$2-3	$3-5
Australia 872 246-7	$4-5	$8-9	$15-18
Holland 872 246-7	$4-5	$8-9	$15-18
Let's Put the X in Sex Hot Urban/Hot Rock Mixes			
PRO694-7DJ			
Mercury Promo label	$6-8	$13-15	$25-30
Hide Your Heart/Betrayed			
USA 876 146-7			
Mercury label	$1-1	$2-3	$3-5
Australia 876 146-7	$1-2	$3-4	$5-8
Germany 876 444-7, censor logo	$1-2	$3-4	$5-8
UK			
KISS 010	$1-2	$3-4	$5-8
KISR-10 red vinyl	$3-4	$6-8	$12-15
Forever/The Street Giveth and the Street Taketh Away			
USA 876 716-7			
Mercury label	$1-1	$2-3	$3-5
Australia 876 716-7	$1-1	$2-3	$3-5
Germany 876 716-7	$1-1	$2-3	$3-5

Item	VG	EX	NM
Germany 876 716-7, censor logo	$1-1	$2-3	$3-5
UK			
KISS 011	$1-2	$3-4	$5-8
KISP 11, patch	$3-4	$6-8	$12-15
Rock and Roll All Nite			
PRO 1086-7 *"It's The Music Stupid"* sleeve			
Mercury promo white label	$9-10	$18-20	$35-40
DVD			
Detroit Rock City	$2-3	$4-5	$7-10
MTV Unplugged	$20-25	$40-50	$80-100
The Second Coming	$5-6	$10-13	$20-25
KISS Immortals (game)	$5-6	$10-13	$20-25
Xtreme Close up	$4-5	$8-10	$15-20
KISS Exposed	$5-6	$10-13	$20-25
KISS My ASS	$4-5	$8-10	$15-20
KISS Symphony	$4-5	$8-10	$15-20
The Best of KISS	$2-3	$4-5	$7-10

An Interview with Bill Aucoin

Former KISS manager shares some memories

What can I say about being able to finally sit down and talk KISS collecting with Bill Aucoin? This is the man who discovered KISS. This is the man who trained and molded KISS into the most entertaining performers in the history of rock 'n' roll. This is the one person I ever wanted to ask about the world of KISS. Quite frankly, this is the only person who can give the world an unvarnished view of KISS from the beginning. As their former manager, he saw the band warts and all, and he calls it like he sees it.

A special thanks to Keith Leroux and Jeff Stouder at www.kissshop.com for setting up this interview at the 2002 Indianapolis KISS Expo.

Tom Shannon: When in the world are you going to write a book about KISS?

Bill Aucoin: I think right now, Sean Delaney is writing one (Author note: Sean has passed away since this interview). I'm helping him with that. I'm not sure that I'm going to right now. I thought I would wait until I was about 80, so I could tell you anything I wanted, and not care.

TS: There is nothing contractually to stop you from doing that now?

BA: No.

TS: I know the world wants to hear your experiences.
BA: It may happen soon, but not for a couple of years yet.

TS: The first appearance for KISS on vinyl as a group appears to be a Warner Brothers promotional compilation set titled "Hard Goods." A gentleman who collects the Warner compilations says that this was the first of 12 such releases in 1974, so it had to be released in January or February. What are your remembrances of this release?
BA: Warner Brothers had a promotional thing obviously when they were going to put out a new artist. Warner Brothers initially gave Neil Bogart the money to start Casablanca, and then they had a falling out, around KISS actually as the falling out happened, because Warner's never thought he should have signed KISS. They thought KISS wasn't a good band; that they'd never make it; that a makeup group was foolish anyway, and that they didn't have that many good songs. In any case, that was why that whole Warner Brothers attachment. Of course every month they would put out a promotional piece, saying basically here's our new acts that are coming out. That's basically what you saw. The album came out in February of '74, and what happened was heads of Warner's actually sent around a memo to their staff saying not to work the record, because they wanted it to die. Well first of all they didn't think it would work anyway, but they wanted it just to die a quick death so they could just tell Neil "Move on, you'll get better acts than this." Neil, by that time, had ties with everyone at Warner Brothers, and someone passed him the memo. He went crazy, went back and said, "Look, I can't work with someone who doesn't believe what I believe." And so what happened was they had an understanding; he

left Warner's and started Casablanca as an independent label. He actually had to mortgage his house and everything else to keep it going. That's how KISS actually kept going. Otherwise, if it had been up to Warner's, they would have killed KISS right there.

TS: "Strutter" seemed like a strange choice to be put on the album, because it was the third release from the debut album.
BA: What do you mean?

TS: I was surprised they didn't use "Nothin' To Lose." I'm assuming they felt that was the most powerful song since they wanted to release it first.
BA: In radio, you ask the promotion people what they think they can work, and "Strutter" was one of those songs.

TS: That leads to another question. Of the three 45 releases for the first LP, it seems that "Strutter," as well as several other songs, was more indicative of the band's sound than "Nothin' To Lose," and certainly more so than "Kissin' Time." It is fairly common knowledge that Neil Bogart, the founder of Casablanca records, forced "Kissin' Time" on the band, but were there particular reasons why "Cold Gin," Deuce," "Firehouse," and "Black Diamond" were passed as singles or B-sides?
BA: One thing is the promotion people. Also it is what radio will play. I think they were hoping to have more of a pop radio rock sound, than they were a harder sound. Ultimately at that time, it was really whatever the promotion department thought they could get away with and get played, more than anything. It was the beginning of

everything, no one really knew. We were having a lot of people fight us. Most radio stations didn't even want to think about playing this makeup band. So it was whatever they thought they could work.

TS: I guess it's easier in hindsight to say which songs are really more the KISS sound.
BA: It had nothing to do with what was their sound or not, so much as what we could get played. Whatever it was that they thought could get played. And don't forget when they put all the money out for the Kissing contest, that's why they did Kissin' Time, although we hated doing it. But, that's how we got it played because they put up so much money for these kissing contests for every radio station.

TS: Speaking of the Warner Brothers distribution deal, was there a noticeable decline in sales at that time that could be traced to that deal no longer being in effect?
BA: No, they really didn't sell that many records at all in the beginning, Tom. Whether it was KISS, or Hotter Than Hell, or Dressed To Kill, it doesn't make any difference. We were selling 30-40,000, maybe 80,000; maybe. So none of those first albums really started selling until the fans started coming back to them afterwards.

TS: You may not be aware of this, but the two most valuable and rare KISS 45s are "Strutter," the last of the Warner-distributed 45s, and "Let Me Go, Rock And Roll," the first 45 distributed by Casablanca. Both were released during the transition period. Was Casablanca up to the task of distributing its own material from 1974 to late1975?
BA: You mean when they left Warner's?

TS: Correct.
BA: No. Neil knew all of the independent distributors. When he was the president of Buddha before he got the Warner's deal, that was all independent, so Neil knew them all. He had a rough time getting money from them. He went to ask them for money to run the label. That was hard, but not the distribution. They readily were willing to do the job.

TS: I'll tell you, if you've got either of those two singles.
BA: (Laughing) How did I know that was coming up?

TS: You should know that two copies of "Strutter" sold in the past week for over $225.
BA: So if I send you a few copies, you'll be ok?

TS: I just wanted to let you know that KISS singles from that era have reached the stratosphere.
BA: I'll remember that.

TS: From the beginning, the band's overseas 45 releases had picture sleeves. Why was America left out, except for "Flaming Youth," during the original makeup era?
BA: That was totally up to the international distributor, whether they wanted to spend the money for that or not. Some of them just didn't feel it was worth it.

TS: Rumors have swirled for years that Alive! was released as a contract fulfillment, and was basically going to end the association

of KISS and Casablanca, true of false?
BA: It wasn't necessarily the end. During Dressed To Kill, the record company didn't have that much money. That's why Neil Bogart produced it. Because it was a real tough financial time, they thought that the easiest thing would be to do a live album. Because of the cost as well as the fact that we weren't selling records so much, but we knew the fans were coming to the shows. So, it just made sense. That was the combination.

TS: I have researched the official RIAA (Recording Industry Association of America) records. How is it possible that Alive is only certified Gold? To this day the RIAA only recognizes 500,000 copies sold, yet the band says over four million.
BA: No, it's over four million.

TS: I believe it is, but that's not what the RIAA says.
BA: We sold almost three (million) way back then.

TS: It's never been recognized by the RIAA.
BA: I've got a platinum record.

TS: It must be an in-house award, not an RIAA. Can I have a picture of it some time?
BA: (Pausing) I'll tell you why not. Because Neil (Bogart) was playing games with a lot of the sales, the RIAA didn't want to recognize it because they knew Neil was. I just remembered that, you've got my memory working now.

TS: Would an RIAA search be initiated and paid for by a band or a record label?
BA: In those days, technically they were supposed to believe what the record company said. Today they don't, they research it. In those days they technically believed what the record company said. Except, again, they knew Neil was a promotion guy and would throw things off more than normal, but generally they would take the word of the record label.

TS: Was there ever a press kit for Alive? I'm a big press kit collector, and I've never seen one.
BA: There had to be, we did one for every album practically, except for the first one I think.

TS: No, there is one for the first one.
BA: There is one for the first one?

TS: There sure is.
BA: Well then, we always did one for every album. There must have been. The only thing that could have hurt that a bit was that was when we were in legal negotiations with Neil over none payment of royalties.

TS: Right.
BA: So there were all sorts of things happening then. But I would have thought we still had one. I'm surprised if we didn't.

TS: Alive II exists as an LP in a very limited number as an error

printing. Three songs, "Take Me," "Hooligan," and "Do You Love Me," are listed on the back cover, but do not appear on the vinyl or labels.
BA: I never knew that until you just told me.

TS: So you don't have any information about that?
BA: No, I have no clue about that. That is completely new to me. I never even realized that.

TS: Rumors again. Rumors exist that on the Dynasty LP.
BA: (laughing) You and your rumors.

TS: I'm just trying to clear some things up.
BA: Go ahead.

TS: Supposedly the band is wearing straight jackets and they were blacked out, true or false?
BA: Yeah.

TS: So that's true?
BA: It wasn't so much blacked out, we just used their heads; remember? The straightjacket pictures never really looked that great. We did them all in straightjackets.

TS: Again on the promotional stuff, to my knowledge there has never appeared a promotional copy of Music From "The Elder." Do you recall if there was one produced?
BA: Well, I think there had to be, only because that was the normal process for a record label. The problem is the record label didn't

believe in the record. I'm sure there were promotional copies, but they probably didn't make very many.

TS: The greatest publicity campaign pulled off in the name of KISS, in my opinion, was the appearance in Cadillac, Michigan.
BA: I agree.

TS: Who decided to do that?
BA: I did. My assistant came in one day with this letter from the football coach of Cadillac High, explaining the problems and what happened. Everyone liked KISS, and could KISS come to the school because they felt that the kids had a lot of apathy and didn't have the excitement they should have in high school. I then built on that. I said there is a possibility, but we have to make it something more exciting. I then came up with the idea of everyone wearing KISS makeup; make it all be one big thing. He went back and checked and said, "Well yeah, if you'll come we'll do that." We went through that process. By the time we actually got there, it had caught on and the whole town was involved. That's why it turned out to be so great. There is a great story about us. I said, "You know, we should land like the Beatles." We didn't have any money in those days. We got a company that had a helicopter. All we could afford is really to have it come up and land, and then go back and land, that was it. So we just barely could afford that. I'll never forget, the helicopter pilot went, bomp (makes hand motion straight up, and straight down). That was it. That was all we could afford. I agree, I think that was one of the, I think that was THE promotion.

TS: It was a beautiful concept. I think every high school fan of KISS from that point on hoped that they could have the same thing happen. On a different subject, Paul has broken a guitar at the end of the show since at least 1976. Did the manufacturers donate the guitars?
BA: No. It cost us $65 apiece. What they would do was, they would agree to take broken parts or whatever they had and make the bodies. There were no real guts to it. Then we would saw the back of it so it would break easy, because Paul couldn't break them. We had a whole truckload we used to get from Gibson at 65 bucks apiece.

TS: So they were defective?
BA: They weren't real. There were no guts to them, no wiring or anything.

TS: Do you recall at what point did Paul start using fire helmets while performing Hotter than Hell?
BA: They had a fire helmet even back when they had started. We then decided to make it a merchandising piece where he could throw it out in the audience, or do whatever.

TS: Any idea why he would not wear one today?
BA: I don't think he wants to mess up his hair (smiling broadly).

TS: A photo of the band out of makeup appeared in the *National Enquirer* in the late '70s, early '80s.
BA: Well, not quite. They had a hand up as I recall, kind of almost, but not quite.

TS: This is even better. It is in the *KISStory* book on page 80. One guy is wearing glasses.
BA: Oh that's it, yeah.

TS: It appears from the combination of earrings and necklaces Peter and Ace were wearing, the photo was taken the same day as the first album cover photo shoot. Anything you can tell me about that photo?
BA: It wouldn't have happened from the first. No one knew who the hell they were, and wouldn't have cared one iota.

TS: Who designed the KISS press kits?
BA: Actually it was a combination of myself and Dennis (Wolloch). He worked at Howard Marks agency. That's how Howard Marks got involved in the first place. I went to his agency to get some artwork done. Dennis would help us design it. I would tell him what I wanted.

TS: Who originated the idea of producing the KISS army kits?
BA: That came through the merchandising company that I had started, that's all. What we did was we looked at all of the fan clubs and stuff. After looking at all of the fan clubs we decided what would kind of work for a KISS army.

TS: There were always a lot of materials in the kits. Were you able to make a profit on them?
BA: Not really, no. That was never really profitable, but all of the other merchandise was. To keep everyone interested, and having the fans, it was worth doing.

TS: I assume you negotiated the licensing agreements while you were with KISS.
BA: Yes.

TS: What was the procedure on that? Were licensees sought out, or did they come to you?
BA: Yes, we sought them out. Of course, then when the manufacturers started realizing for themselves, they then would come. I would then say, "Give me a prototype." Then if I liked the prototype it would go back and forth. Then when I thought it was good enough, I would bring it to the group and say, "Here, do you like it, or don't you like it," or "any changes." Then I would go back and give them approval or not, depending on what we felt.

TS: After Alive was released with the booklet insert, Destroyer came out with no inserts, unless you count the high quality lyric sleeve. From that point on all releases included cool inserts. Who came up with the concept of doing that?
BA: I wanted to do that for a reason. Neil, and no one else wanted to do that. It was a little expensive to do, but we had a lot of bootleg problems. They could snap those covers and press those albums out as soon as you had them out, but the bootleggers couldn't afford to do the merchandising pieces. Any kids had to know if you got one without it, you either got one that was a mishap, which was not usually the case, so you usually got a bootleg; that's how we could tell the difference.

TS: So you had a lot of trouble convincing the label to do it?

BA: Oh yeah. It was a lot more expensive. Not only just to make the merchandising piece, but to insert it. The pressing plants would charge you for everything that went in. An extra couple of cents, or whatever it was just to take that and put it in. So the cost, it was expensive.

TS: Who paid for the inserts?
BA: The record label did. That's why they didn't want it. Neil would call and say, "Bill, do you think you can do without the merchandising piece this time around?"
TS: I'm glad you didn't. That's probably one of the things that is responsible for the band still being popular today. The Originals was distributed promotionally. There are very rare versions floating around in collecting circles with white promotional labels, and cut corners on the cover. Since this was a re-release of the first three LPs, and was probably not going to garner additional radio play, to whom were the promotional copies intended to be distributed?
BA: See the promotional copies were just a regular routine with any label. So you did it so the promotions guys could carry it, and give it to people and hope that something might come out of it. It was kind of a regular routine, that's all. You have the marketing department, and the department that handled that, and a record label would just do that automatically. You have something come out, you order 500 of this. It just would happen, that's all.

TS: I purchased my personal copy of the promotional edition of The Originals around 1992 at a record show in Cincinnati. When I arrived at the show at midday, the dealer had 13 near-mint copies

remaining. The sight of those LPs was mind-boggling. The Originals, as a general rule, is extremely susceptible to ring wear because of the thin black cover used to hold all of the materials. I have never seen a near-mint stock copy, although I am sure they exist. These were so nice that I was concerned they were counterfeit. I asked him how he found so many copies.
BA: He probably had a whole box of them.

TS: In fact, he did. He said that the week before a buddy of his who worked for Warner Brothers had found a case of the albums in a Warner warehouse in California. My question is, why would Warner Brothers have had these LPs? The distribution deal was long past. Since KISS was included in the set, would Casablanca have been required to give some of the promo copies to Warner Brothers because of the long expired distribution deal?
BA: It might have been a warehouse that handled independent stock as well. That's not unusual. You might have one of the distributors that handled independents and majors.

TS: Why was The Originals II never released anywhere except Japan?
BA: I think just because Japan wanted it. Don't forget, if one of the distributors says, "I think we can do well with this. Can we put this out? We did well with the first Originals, can we do it again" fine, but I don't think we thought in the States that it was that strong. Again, it was a copy, of a copy, of a copy again. God knows we put out songs over, and over, and over.

TS: Once the band began to be marketed to a younger audience, were

there any real objections from the band members?
BA: It wasn't really intended to, the younger generation just caught up to the band is all. We never really tried to market to them. That was one of the things that Paul hated, and one of the reasons he wanted to take off the makeup, and he didn't want to do any more merchandising. It just ran into the next generation. There's nothing you could do about it. I said, "You just keep going, they will grow with it." They didn't like that at all.

TS: I wonder how they feel about it now, because if you look around now, many of the collectors and fans are 30-35 years old, the same six- to 12-year-old kids from 1978.
BA: Oh, they love it now.

TS: One of the rarest and most valuable pieces of KISS concert memorabilia is the original Dynasty tour program. Everyone is familiar with the more common versions with the Dynasty LP artwork on the front. The rare version is worth at least $1,200 in near-mint condition. It is titled, "The Return of KISS," and features the band in front of the New York skyline. How long was it produced, and why was it halted? Was it because of the multiple dates listed for many cities in the front of the book that never materialized?
BA: I remember that something had to be changed; the guys didn't like this photo somehow, or maybe I didn't or something. That I didn't think it was strong enough, or something. I can't remember what had to be changed, but we found either an error inside or something, and as long as we were redoing it, we wanted something stronger.

TS: What is the story behind the famous poster of the band way up over the city of New York?
BA: The guys were scared to death. We were up on top of the Empire State building. There was a little metal platform that was attached to the side of the building to take background pictures for the King Kong movie. It was big enough because those old movie cameras were huge back in those days. They had to mount the camera on that, so it was a substantial platform, but it was hanging on the side of the building. Someone told me about it, and we actually got the guys to go out on the little platform, and we got the shot.

TS: You have been very kind answering all of these questions. I have two specific things I need to ask you. On Page 116 of my book, *Goldmine Kiss Collectibles Price Guide*, are pictures of what are artists' proofs from the wheels of custom slot machines that were reportedly given to you and the members of KISS by Neil Bogart. Did you ever receive such a machine, and are these the artwork from the wheels?
BA: Yes, I still have the machine packed away. Neil had them made for the band, and one for me.

TS: Would you describe it?
BA: It's an old-time slot machine with a wooden base, and an old heavy metal pull handle, one of the original slot machines. It was painted with blue and red and then obviously when you pulled it you got the three logos or faces.

TS: I think your machine had the best wheel pictures, because yours was the only on that had all four guys faces on it. Last question.
BA: One last question, OK!

TS: If you were managing KISS today, what would be your assessment of their current status, and what direction would you lead them?
BA: I wouldn't have put out Psycho Circus until they had a great album with at least one or two songs that were for radio airplay. I think they could have waited another year. They had such a success from the reunion tour, which I knew would happen, that until you were ready to do something great, that you knew worked, I wouldn't have done that. In the reunion tour they did a copy of the show we put together back in '78, but they let everything be seen. My philosophy about any of the gimmicks we used was, you don't see them until it's time. I was really disappointed in that, like the cranes they had on stage. The idea of doing a show is that you don't know what's going to happen until it happens. A lot of the stuff that they did was very obvious and I thought it wasn't done right. Also, as a slight aside, I told Gene when he tried to spit blood that the blood was too thick. I said, "Gene you didn't handle the blood right." "What are you talking about Bill?" he said. I said, "You never knew this, but the blood we used, we always diluted it 50 percent, so that when you did that it would go everywhere. You don't remember that, do you?" "Uh, no." That's why it kind of dribbled out of his mouth, and really never came out. He had forgotten. There were a lot of things we used to do for them that we never even told them. We just made it work behind the scenes. One of the key elements I told everyone at Aucoin

Management was, everything we do you keep quiet about, because everything should always seem like it comes from the band. I think that's the way it should be.

Now I think they are getting a little tired, and they are going to milk it as long as they can. The only thing that I think would be terrific would be if they were willing to work with other really good writers, kind of not own it all themselves, but write with other writers. Wouldn't it be great if after all these years that they came out with a really great rock and roll album? That's the only thing they haven't done since they got back together. I would say whatever it takes. Let's hire the best writers; let's get together with the best producers, even if we have to do 10 producers. Let's come out with an album that can be so good it will be a classic and sell millions and millions. Then it would really conclude your career, it would bring everything together again.

Price guide

Action figures, 30-54
Advertisements, full-page magazine, 54, 55, 56
Air fresheners, 54
Arcade dolls, 57, 58
Ashtrays, 57
Autographs, 57

Baby supplies, 57
Backpacks, 59
Back stage passes, 60
Bags, 61
Baseballs, 62
Balloons, 63
Bandanas, 64
Bean Bag Toys, 65
Bears, 65, 66
Bedspread, 67
Beer can, Czechoslovakia, 68
Belt, 69
Belt buckles, 69-71
Bendies/superposables, 71
Blanket/throw, 71
Bobble heads, 72, 73
Books, 73-77
    Songbooks, 77-86
Boxes, LP and cassette storage, 86
Busts, 87-88
Calendars, 89-90
Camera, disposable, 91
Candy dispenser, 92
Cards, collector, 93-98
Cars and trucks, die cast, 98-111
Casket, 111
CD-ROM, 111, 112
Chair, inflatable, 113
Christmas ornaments, ball style, 114
Clocks, 114
Coins, sets, 114, 115, 117
Colorforms, 116, 117
Comics, 117-120
Condoms, 121, 122
Credit cards, 123
Cups, plastic, 124, 125

Doormats, 124, 125
Drumsticks, 124, 126-127

Fireman's helmets, 127-128

Games, 128, 129
Glassware, 128, 130-133
Glitter lamp, 133, 134
Golf equipment, 133, 135
Gruntz, 133, 136
Guitars and equipment, member endorsed, 1367-145
Guitar picks, 146-157
Guitar pickups (mini guitar), 158, 159
Guitar strap, strings, picks, 158, 160
Guitar/toy, 158, 161

Halloween costumes, 158
Halloween helmet mask, 158
Hats, 162
Headliners (mini big head figurines), 162, 163, 164

Incense sticks, 164
Incense burners, 164
Ink pens, 165-166

Jersey, 166
Jewelry, 166-168
Jump suit, crewmember, 168

Key chain, 168-170
KISS ARMY kits, 170

KISS Army News, 170, 171

Lava lamp, 170, 173
License plate, 172, 173
License plate frame, 172
Light string, 172, 173
Lighter, disposable, 172
Lighter, refillable, 172, 174
Lunch box/drink containers, 174-178

Makeup kit, 178-180
Magazines, 181-228
Magnets, 228-230
Models, 230-231
Mouse pads, 232, 233

N The Box (Jack in the box), 233, 234
Notebooks, 233, 235, 236

Pajamas, 237
Pencils, 238
PEZ Dispensers (bootleg), 240
Phone cards, 239, 240
Photographs, official sets, 241-243
Pillows, 244, 245
Pillowcases, 244, 246
Pinball machine, 244
Pins, 247-251
Plates, 252
Pool cues, 252
Poster art, 252, 253, 254
Posters, 255-264
Poster put ons, 264
Promotional items, 264-291

Radio, 291, 292
Record Awards, RIAA, 293-294
Record player, 294
Robe, 295

Scarves, 295, 296
Scream machine, 295, 297
Script (not photo copied), 298
Shirts, 298-303
Shoelaces, 303, 304, 305
Skateboard, 305
Sleeping bag, 305, 306
Slippers, 305, 307
Snow globes, 305, 308, 309
Statues, 310
Stickers, 311-313

Telephone, 313
Tickets, 314-316
Ties, 316-317
Tour programs/tour books 318-338
Towels, beach, 339, 340
Trashcan, 339, 341

Umbrella, 339
Underoos, 339

Van, radio control, 339
View-Master, 339, 342
Videotapes, official, 342-344

Wine, 344
Wristband, 345

Yo-Yo, 345

American and selected foreign music

Foreign 12" singles, 355-359
Pre-KISS releases, 345

Promo CD singles, 359-360
Promo-only, 346-354
Radio shows, 360-363
USA promo 12" singles, 354-355

Albums

30 Anõs De Musica Rock, 397, 401
Ace Frehley, 383
Alive!, 12, 14, 365, 366, 367, 368
Alive II, 17, 376, 377, 378, 379
Alive III, 409, 411, 412, 413
Animalize, 22, 403
Asylum, 22, 403
Best of KISS, The, 424
Best of KISS Volume 2, The, 424
Best of Solo Albums, 384, 385, 386, 387
Box Set, The, 423-424
Carnival of Souls: The Final Sessions, 417
Chikara, 407, 408
Con Todo El Poder De La Musica, 397, 402
Crazy Nights, 22, 407
Creatures of the Night, 20, 392
Destroyer, 14, 369, 370
Double Platinum, 16, 17, 380
Dressed to Kill, 365
Dynasty, 18, 19, 384, 388
Gene Simmons, 380
Greatest Hits, 380, 417, 418
Greatest KISS, 413, 414, 415, 416, 417
The Guitar Technique of Ace Frehley/KISS, 380, 381
Hot in the Shade, 22, 409
Hotter Than Hell, 364-365
Hotter Than Metal, 392, 395
Killers, 392, 393, 394
KISS, 8, 13, 364
KISS Collection: box set, The, 392, 398
KISS Gold, 424
KISS the Singles, 403, 406
KISS: The Very Best of, 424
Lick it Up, 20, 397, 399, 400
Lo Mejor De KISS, 380, 382
Love Gun, 15, 17, 372
Music from "The Elder," 20, 389, 391
MTV Unplugged, 24, 411
O' Rock De KISS, 403, 404
Originals, The, 14, 369, 371
Originals II, The, 372, 375, 376
Originals 1974-1978, The, 419
Originals 1974-1979, The, 419, 420, 422
Paul Stanley, 383
Peter Criss, 383
Psycho Circus, 24, 419, 421, 422
Psycho Circus + Live EP, 423
Revenge, 409, 410
Rockanroleando Toda La Noche, 403, 405
Rock and Roll Over, 14, 372, 373, 374
Smashes, Thrashes and Hits, 21, 22, 407
Smashes, Thrashes and Hits: 15 Years of KISStory, 407
Solo album box set, 383, 385, 387

Superstar, 392, 396
Unmasked, 19, 388-389, 390
You Wanted the Best... You've Got the Best!, 23, 24, 411, 413

45 singles and extended plays

2000 MAN/I Was Made For Lovin' You/Sure Know, 459, 462
A World Without Heroes/ Dark Light, 471
A World Without Heroes/ Mr. Blackwell, 467, 477
All Hell's Breakin' Loose/ Young and Wasted, 486
Beth/Beth-mono/Stereo-Beth, 438
Beth/Detroit Rock City, 438
Beth/Hard Luck Woman, 482
Calling Dr. Love/Take Me, 438
Christine Sixteen/Shock Me, 440, 444
C'mon And Love Me/Getaway, 426, 433, 434
Crazy, Crazy Nights/No, No, No, 487
Creatures of the Night/ Rock and Roll All Nite (Live), 475, 482
Detroit Rock City/Beth, 432
Dirty Livin'/Sure Know Something, 462
Don't You Let Me Down/ Hooked on Rock and Roll, 452, 454
Flaming Youth/God of Thunder, 432
Forever/The Street Giveth and the Street Taketh Away, 488
Hard Luck Woman/ Calling Dr. Love/Beth, 438, 439
Hard Luck Woman/Mr. Speed, 438
Hold Me, Touch Me/ Goodbye, 454
Killers/I Love It Loud, 482
Kissin' Time/Nothing to Lose, 425
Heaven's on Fire/Lonely is the Hunter, 486
Hide Your Heart/Betrayed, 481, 488
I Love It Loud/Danger, 488
I Love It Loud/Killers, 471
I/The Oath, 468, 469, 470, 477
I Was Made For Lovin' You/Hard Times, 453, 457
I Was Made for Lovin' You/Rock and Roll All Nite, 482
Let Me Go, Rock and Roll/Hotter Than Hell, 426, 430
Let's Put the X in Sex/ Calling Dr. Love, 480, 488
Let's Put the X in Sex Hot Urban/Hot Rock Mixes, 488
Lick It Up/Charisma/I Was Made For Lovin' You/Detroit Rock City, 478, 486
Lick It Up/Dance All Over Your Face, 486
Lick It Up/Not for the Innocent, 486
Love Gun/Hooligan, 444

Magic Touch/Save Your Love, 464, 471
New York Groove/Snow Blind, 451, 454
Nothin' To Lose/Kissin' Time/Strutter/Deuce, 425, 429
Nothin' To Lose/Love Theme From KISS, 425, 427, 428
Radioactive/Hold Me Touch Me/New York Groove/Don't You Let Me Down, 449, 450
Radioactive/See You in Your Dreams, 454
Reason to Live/Thief in the Night, 487
Rock and Roll All Nite, 489
Rock and Roll All Nite/ Getaway, 426, 431
Rock and Roll All Nite - Live/Studio, 426, 432
Rock and Roll All Nite/ Two Timer/C'mon and Love Me/Anything for My Baby, 432
Rocket Ride/Tomorrow and Tonight, 442, 443
Shandi/Mr. Make Believe/ Firehouse/Rock and Roll All Nite, 471
Shandi/She's So European, 460, 462, 471
Shout It Out Loud (live)/Nothin' To Lose, 441, 444
Shout It Out Loud/Sweet Pain, 432
Star Trax: Rock and Roll All Nite/Shout It Out Loud/Love Gun/Sure Know Something, 458, 462
Strutter/100,000 Years, 425
Strutter '78/Let Me Go, Rock and Roll/Love Gun/Beth, 445, 449
Strutter '78/Shock Me, 446, 447, 448, 449
Sure Know Something/ Dirty Livin', 455, 457, 462
Talk To Me/She's So European, 465, 471
Tears Are Falling/Any Way You Slice It, 487
Thrills in the Night/Burn Bitch Burn, 486
Tomorrow/Is That You, 466, 477
Tomorrow/Naked City, 477
Turn on the Night/Hell or High Water, 487
Uh! All Night/Trial By Fire, 479, 487
You Still Matter to Me/ Hooked on Rock and Roll, 457

DVDs

Best of KISS, The, 485, 489
Detroit Rock City, 489
Exposed, 483
KISS Exposed, 489
KISS Immortals, 489
KISS My ASS, 489
KISS Symphony, 484, 489
MTV Unplugged, 489
Second Coming, The, 489
Xtreme Close Up, 489